A National Strategy for Containing White-Collar Crime

The Battelle Human Affairs Research Centers Series

The White-Collar Challenge to Nuclear Safeguards
by Herbert Edelhertz and *Marilyn Walsh*

Government Requirements of Small Business
by Roland J. Cole and *Philip D. Tegeler*

Third-World Poverty
edited by William Paul McGreevey

National Strategy for Containing White-Collar Crime
edited by Herbert Edelhertz and *Charles Rogovin*

Nuclear Power and the Public
by Stanley Nealey

A National Strategy for Containing White-Collar Crime

Edited by
Herbert Edelhertz
Charles Rogovin
The Battelle Human Affairs
Research Centers

LexingtonBooks
D.C. Heath and Company
Lexington, Massachusetts
Toronto

Library of Congress Cataloging in Publication Data

Main entry under title:

A National strategy for containing white-collar crime.

   Based on a symposium held at the Battelle Seattle Research Center July
20–21, 1978.
   1.   White collar crimes—United States—Prevention—Congresses.
I.   Edelhertz, Herbert.   II.   Rogovin, Charles H.
HV6695.N38   364.1'68   79-2373
ISBN 0-669-03166-6

Copyright © 1980 by D.C. Heath and Company

Published simultaneously in Canada

Printed in the United States of America

International Standard Book Number: 0-669-03166-6

Library of Congress Catalog Card Number: 79-2373

To Amy and Ruth

Contents

Preface and Acknowledgments

Crime is dealt with primarily by local law-enforcement agencies. Though major publicity in the national media tends to focus on federal law enforcement, most criminal cases are detected, investigated, and prosecuted at municipal and county levels. One class of cases, "white-collar" or "economic" crime, has been traditionally regarded as a federal area because most attention has been given to major mail frauds, securities frauds, banking violations, and frauds against the federal government. This focus on cases of national interest has served to obscure the day-in, day-out involvement of local prosecutors in efforts to contain white-collar crime—an involvement that has traditionally been low profile but constant in most parts of the United States. Governmental efforts that are low profile, no matter how important, also tend to be low priority for obtaining resources; hence the need for special attention to this area of local law-enforcement responsibility.

Beginning in 1973, a group of local prosecutors moved forcefully to promote local white-collar-crime-enforcement efforts and to move them to the forefront of local prosecutive attention. The Economic Crime Committee was established in the National District Attorneys Association (NDAA) to take the place of a committee that had earlier focused on narrower consumer-protection issues. This move was clearly an unusual one for NDAA, which, like most organizations in the law-enforcement field, was accustomed to addressing more traditional criminal challenges, such as violent crime and property crimes.

Particularly noteworthy about this organizational thrust was that it developed at a time when street crimes were a major public concern, one that was reflected by the priority that political candidates gave to the street-crime issue in federal, state, and local campaigns. In 1973 financial demands for street-crime containment left little in the way of resources for other prosecutive crime-control initiatives.

At the heart of this new prosecutive thrust was the perception that white-collar-criminal behavior was "crime" in the same sense as street crime, that law-enforcement credibility in dealing with street criminals depended on even-handed attention to theft—regardless of the social status or *modus operandi* of the offender. Institutionally, prosecutors had finally recognized that the existing federal effort was necessarily a selective one that by its very nature and organization could not adequately respond to local white-collar-crime-containment requirements. The federal government clearly did not have the prosecutive manpower in U.S. Attorneys' offices to do so and could not set policies and priorities to meet a multitude of local concerns.

The NDAA Economic Crime Committee persisted in its effort to organize a prosecutors' movement to convince both the national prosecutive community and the public that white-collar-crime containment was an appropriate and necessary operational area for the local prosecutor and to find resources that could help them to do so. This led to discussions among the committee, the Academy for Contemporary Problems in Columbus, Ohio, and the Battelle Law and Justice Study Center in Seattle, Washington, which produced an action plan that gained the support of the Law Enforcement Assistance Administration (LEAA) for the NDAA Economic Crime Project.

This action plan for an Economic Crime Project had two major objectives: to enhance the capabilities of local prosecutors to deal with white-collar crime and to establish white-collar-crime containment within the normative framework of local prosecutors' responsibilities. It was inevitable that efforts in these directions would in turn focus attention on new issues that would go beyond the original objectives of the Economic Crime Project.

Once consciously part of the white-collar-crime-containment network, prosecutors have been forced to consider how our nation's resources, federal and nonfederal, can best be mobilized to deal with white-collar crime and related abuses. As part of this same inquiry, other important and broader issues emerge naturally, involving the roles and utility of criminal, civil, administrative, regulatory, and private-sector processes in white-collar-crime containment.

In the almost five years of its operation, from 1973 to 1978, the NDAA's Economic Crime Project had made substantial progress toward achieving its original objectives, but it felt compelled to address these broader issues, which are strategic rather than tactical in character. At the same time similar concerns were being felt at federal levels, particularly in the Criminal Division of the Department of Justice. In many quarters there was growing perception of the need for a national strategy to deal with white-collar crime. The NDAA Economic Crime Project, with the support and encouragement of the Adjudication Division of the Office of Criminal Justice Programs of the LEAA, therefore commissioned the Battelle Law and Justice Study Center to conduct a small but broadly based symposium to consider the issues involved in developing and implementing a national strategy. The symposium was held at the Battelle Seattle Research Center on 20–21 July 1978.

This book deals primarily with the proceedings of the symposium, but against the backdrop of the issues that were its genesis. It goes on to consider the impact of the symposium in terms of its effect on white-collar-crime containment. It is rarely possible to see operational improvements or changes clearly flowing from symposium papers and discussion; in this instance, however, that relationship is quite clear. The report of the symposium and its papers were, in a very real sense, a resource and a guide for law enforcement and U.S. Congressional Committee deliberations on how to structure and implement white-collar-crime-containment activities. Finally, the book considers future strategic options and alternatives in the field of white-collar-crime containment.

Many individuals and organizations contributed to this book, directly or through their efforts in support of the symposium that is its core. We hope that we may be forgiven by any contributors we have inadvertently overlooked. First, we recognize the support of NDAA through its former president, Lee C. Falke, prosecuting attorney for Montgomery County (Dayton, Ohio); former-prosecutor Robert F. Leonard of Genesee County (Flint, Michigan), then chairman of the NDAA Economic Crime Committee; Patrick F. Healy, former executive director of NDAA; and James P. Heelan of the NDAA staff. Second, we note the support of the Adjudication Division of the Office of Criminal Justice Programs, LEAA, and the personal participation in the symposium of the division's chief, James C. Swain. Third, we gratefully acknowledge the contributions of Professor Mark H. Moore of Harvard University, Daniel L. Skoler of the American Bar Association, and William A. Morrill of Mathematica Policy Research, each of whom prepared the papers that were the starting points for the symposium discussions. Fourth, we owe a very special debt of gratitude to all the participants who joined with us in the symposium as concerned citizens and as representatives of public and private agencies that spanned federal and local prosecution functions, the federal inspector-general function, regulatory agencies, a state attorney general's office, and a consumer-protection organization.

Finally, we are most grateful for the many contributions of the Battelle Human Affairs Research Centers staff. Dr. Marilyn Walsh and Dr. Mary McGuire of the Battelle Law and Justice Study Center were important contributors to the group that planned the symposium and were the rapporteurs for its first and second sessions. Frederic A. Morris of the Science and Government Center served as rapporteur of the third session. Bert H. Hoff of the Battelle Law and Justice Study Center was of particular assistance in tracing and chronicling the activities that followed and were influenced by the symposium. Scott Coplan, a research assistant in the Battelle Law and Justice Study Center, served as coordinator and one-man secretariat for this entire effort and made major contributions to the preparation and editing of the contents of this book; Donna Randall, also a research assistant in the Center, unobtrusively but very effectively provided all those elements of support that are essential to the smooth workings of any meeting. Ingrid

McCormack and Cheryl Osborn of the Center staff prepared the numerous drafts of papers and invaluable secretarial support that is the basis for any successful project and, together with Charleen Duitsman, handled all the typing and technical aspects of preparing the manuscript of this book for publication. Last, we express our appreciation to the staff of the Battelle Conference Center in Seattle for the care they gave to every detail involving the physical setting for the symposium and the accommodations provided for its participants.

**Part I
The Need for a National
Strategy to Contain
White-Collar Crime**

1 Introduction

White-collar crime is a pervasive form of antisocial behavior that must be countered by a broad range of responses and remedies provided by agencies in both the public and the private sectors. In the former these responses include investigation, prosecution, regulation, and administrative measures to prevent and detect such crime. In the private sector, responses are available through certain forms of industry self-regulation (sometimes under the prodding and monitoring of regulatory agencies such as the SEC's monitoring of the securities industry's self-regulation), by internal corporate-security departments, and by the ever-present prospect of stockholders' derivative actions that can be occasioned by high-level corporate mismanagement, negligence, or deliberate wrongdoing.

Much discussion has revolved around the definition of "white-collar crime." The concern about the definition is understandable because the words have no clear meaning. To some the term is inextricably linked to the (high social) status of the offender;[1] to others it is a description of particular behavior or *modi operandi*.[2] For purposes of this book the latter construction is adopted, possibly because of the personal convictions of the authors but more important because this approach is consistent with the approach taken by those in the enforcement community who recognize the need for development and implementation of a national strategy to deal with white-collar crime. Attorney General Benjamin Civiletti, for example, addressed this issue in testimony to the U.S. Congress:

> Our definition markedly departs from the traditional view held by many sociologists who have in the past stressed the social characteristics of the offender or the relationship between offenders and their occupations. That traditional academic approach does not accurately reflect the types of offenses and offenders encountered by the criminal justice system. . . . The traditional approach was further rejected because it implicitly raises the spector [sic] of large enforcement agencies targeting whole segments of society for special enforcement emphases—the innocent along with the guilty—a notion which is repugnant to our sense of fair play and equal protection under the law.[3]

The definition that has been adopted for use by the National District Attorneys Association (NDAA) Economic Crime Project, and characterized by the U.S. Department of Justice as a "good working definition,"[4] is the following:

3

[White-collar crime is] . . . an illegal act or series of illegal acts committed by non-physical means and by concealment or guile, to obtain money or property, to avoid the loss of money or property, or to obtain business or personal advantage. [5]

The boundaries of this definition necessarily are vague. Clearly, it would cover a conventional con game or outright consumer fraud. Much definitional confusion arises where criminal schemes involve some mixture of white-collar crime and more conventional or traditional crime. For example, the theft of stock certificates from a brokerage house is hardly a white-collar crime in and of itself, but marketing the security through its use as loan collateral would involve a whole range of behavior coming within the preceding definition. The buyer for a department store would not, under this definition, commit a white-collar crime in taking a bribe or kickback for purchasing stolen merchandise on behalf of his employer, but he would be engaging in white-collar-criminal behavior toward his unwitting employer.

The problem of dealing with white-collar crime is further compounded by the fact that there is no clear separation between criminal, civil, and regulatory responses. Precisely the same behavior may be, and often is, subject to the same remedies. For example, the decision to prosecute a securities fraud criminally or a banking violation criminally will depend relatively more on the prosecutor's evaluation of the evidence than on the inherent characteristics of the behavior being assessed. Unlike street crime or conventional property theft where the questions for law-enforcement authorities are what happened and who was responsible, in this area the question is whether there is sufficient proof of wrongful intent to warrant criminal prosecution even where what happened and who caused it to happen are not in dispute. In white-collar cases there are usually noncriminal alternatives available that make it easier to decline criminal prosecution, for example, civil action, regulatory agency action, administrative measures, and private litigation. Such actions can be undertaken by victims if they have personal resources to launch the efforts or can make it attractive for private counsel to enlist in their causes on a contingent-fee basis.

The existence of these alternatives also increases the likelihood that behavior that should be prosecuted will not be if it comes first to the attention of an agency that does not have criminal jurisdiction or that has some other primary objective such as revenue collection, recovery of funds, or promotion of the economic health of an industry being regulated. This is the problem of overlapping authority, to which we now turn.

Overlapping authority is present at all stages of containment efforts: detection, investigation, criminal prosecution, civil litigation, and adjudication. This is clear from examination of any one of a number of classic white-collar crime schemes such as embezzlement, frauds against government programs, consumer fraud, or securities fraud.

Each of these schemes are proscribed by both federal and state law. They can therefore be investigated and prosecuted by federal, state, or local agencies and can be adjudicated in either federal or state courts. By whom they will be investigated or prosecuted will largely depend on how they are detected and on agency policies rather than on the presence or absence of jurisdiction or legal competence to investigate or prosecute. This can best be illustrated by considering bank embezzlement—a crime under federal and state law. Federal statutes require that all embezzlements detected in federally insured banks be promptly reported to the Federal Bureau of Investigation (FBI). The Department of Justice thus has the first option to investigate or prosecute, but this option does not mean that a local prosecutor is without legal power to order an investigation and then to prosecute. Traditionally, however, local law-enforcement agencies defer to federal agencies in this field because violations are being dealt with by competent (federal) authorities, and there would be no point in duplicating the effort. The system appeared to work over the years, though we have no way of knowing how many cases were not prosecuted because U.S. attorneys inappropriately declined action, and such cases went unaddressed because they were regarded as "federal business."

Overlapping authority in the white-collar-crime field has not stimulated conflict, as might have been expected. Agencies have only rarely competed with each other for jurisdiction over "turf" or classes of violations. On the contrary, overlapping authority has had a soporific effect on agencies that have seen others take responsibility for particular areas of enforcement. This arguably explains the anguish, in 1979, when the Department of Justice and the FBI embarked on their "quality prosecution" program. Attorney General Civiletti described this program as follows:

> The Department of Justice has chosen as a matter of policy to focus our resources primarily on those cases which are perceived to have maximum impact and deterrent value. In furtherance of this approach the FBI has adopted a "quality over quantity" program to ensure that major cases are afforded maximum investigative priority.[6]

The side-effects of this "quality over quantity" approach, however, have been to spotlight problems created by unmonitored patterns of overlapping authority. To implement that new program, the FBI developed guidelines that provided, for example, that it would decline to undertake investigations of bank embezzlements below certain fixed-dollar amounts; U.S. attorneys took parallel and consistent positions. This meant that a massive investigative and prosecutive burden was shifted from federal shoulders to local police and to local prosecutors and their investigators. The alternative to local assumption of responsibility would be to create an enforcement vacuum with respect to all bank embezzlements under the guideline amounts. Local prosecutors therefore had to shoulder this burden, with no new resources. This one episode initially generated much conflict and hostility between the Department of Justice and local prosecutors, but happily both groups have worked assiduously to resolve this problem. Nevertheless, the episode served to illustrate the fact that white-collar-crime containment poses an exceedingly complex challenge and that the patterns of overlapping authority in any specific enforcement area should be carefully examined before any changes in enforcement policy are initiated. One agency's unilateral priority-setting exercise can play havoc with the carefully structured and budgeted operations of other agencies with overlapping jurisdictions.

In addition to jurisdiction, white-collar-crime-containment efforts are divided along functional lines that constitute another axis along which issues of overlapping authority must be examined. Divisions along jurisdictional lines are created by legal powers to detect, investigate, and prosecute that exist simultaneously at federal, state, and local levels. There is also a de facto power to investigate in the private sector. Divisions along functional lines relate to the simultaneous operations and responsibilities of specific agencies.

The problem of overlapping jurisdiction is further complicated by the fact that many federal, state, and local agencies have a broad range of functions, for example, a prosecutor often directs investigations and in making prosecutive decisions will consider the impact of what he does on deterrence or prevention.

If one examines a typical white-collar scheme such as the fraudulent sale of business franchises, these patterns of overlapping authority along the axes of jurisdiction and function may easily be seen as follows.

1. There are possible violations under a broad range of federal statutes, including those that proscribe mail fraud, wire fraud, securities fraud, the transportation across state lines of monies obtained by fraud, and the Federal Trade Commission (FTC) Act. Investigations can be undertaken by the U.S. Postal Inspection Service, the FBI, the Securities Exchange Commission (SEC), or the FTC, as well as by a U.S. attorney in an investigative grand jury. The SEC or the FTC can seek regulatory adjudication through their own processes or by recourse to courts for injunctive relief to protect investors; the U.S. attorney can initiate criminal prosecution through a presentation to a federal grand jury.

2. There are possible violations under a broad range of state statutes, including those that proscribe securities fraud, false pretenses, and larceny. Investigation could be undertaken by local consumer-protection agencies, by state attorneys general or local prosecutors, by state agencies regulating

the sale of securities, or by local police agencies. Criminal prosecutions could be initiated by county prosecutors and in some instances by state attorneys general. The state attorney general or the state securities administrator can seek cease-and-desist orders or other injunctive relief; civil actions for restitution of funds to victims can sometimes be initiated by state attorneys general and in some jurisdictions by county prosecutors.

3. There are narrower ranges of potential violations under local laws, for example, those that require licensing for sales and business solicitations. These may be investigated by city consumer-protection agencies and then referred for criminal prosecution to the county prosecutor or to a city attorney.

4. Initial investigations may be undertaken by private agencies such as Better Business Bureaus or other trade organizations, or victims' attorneys may make preliminary investigations and then refer their findings to federal, state, or local agencies for further investigation or prosecution.

Overlapping authority or jurisdiction over white-collar crime and related abuses poses a number of very special problems in addition to those already suggested. First, there is the danger that what is everybody's business becomes no one's business; that much criminal behavior will "fall between the cracks." Second, there is potential waste and conflict arising out of duplication of effort when an area of crime is addressed without adequate coordination; duplication of effort can be constructive or destructive. Third, the allocation of resources to cope with particular white-collar-criminal behavior is rarely related to the significance or impact of the crime.

This third point merits special attention in considering the development of a rational and effective national strategy to contain white-collar crime. If one were to develop accurate measures of the impact of white-collar crimes and related abuses and of the resources expended to contain such behavior at all jurisdictional levels by all agencies, any positive correlations between them would probably by accidental. Federal, state, local, and private efforts to deal with white-collar crime are fragmented along agency and departmental lines and responsive to both conceptual and competitive approaches at these jurisdictional levels. Thus at the federal level it is far easier for prosecutors to decide to devote a substantial percentage of their resources to white-collar crime and related abuses than it is for a local prosecutor. Local officials can do the same thing but only in the face of community and voter demands to cope with violent crimes that directly affect the immediate safety of their constituencies. This is not to say that the federal prosecutor does not face competitive demands, albeit of a different character—the inventory of a U.S. attorney's responsibilities is long and must be dealt with by a staff list that is almost invariably uncomfortably short.

When one looks behind the operations of prosecutors' offices, which are most visible to the public, the anomalies at the detection and investigative level are even more unsettling. For example, vast federal sums are expended locally on a long list of welfare and benefit programs, many of which involved a mixture of federal and state monies. Medicaid programs are a typical example. There is mutual federal-state-local interest in containing frauds against such programs but little in the way of coordinated effort to do so. Some federal monies have been made available to support state efforts in the Medicaid fraud area. By and large, however, the response to such fraud reflects 50 different state policies, resources allocated as a consequence of 50 different levels of concern over the problem, both complicated by a general lack of coordination between federal and state efforts—notwithstanding clear mutuality of interest.

The issue of overlapping authority just described and of uncoordinated efforts in the face of common federal-state-local problems has been characteristic of the white-collar-crime-containment scene for many decades. In major part these difficulties are inherent in our federal system. Why then is there a new and strong perception of the need for a national strategy that will point toward the rational deployment of governmental and private resources to deal with white-collar crime? The answers are probably to be found in a number of relatively recent developments and in a rising consciousness of the need to improve containment responses on the part of law-enforcement professionals.

These relatively new developments are the rise of the consumer movement, new public awareness of white-collar-crime issues, increased capability to utilize the techniques of white-collar-crime investigation and prosecution, proliferating public welfare and benefit programs vulnerable to abuse, and special applicability of white-collar-crime investigative and prosecutive techniques to enforcement areas as diverse as organized crime and environmental protection. Mounting levels of taxation stimulate increased concern about fraud, waste, and abuse in government programs. We fear the development of new technologies of crime such as the use of the computer as a tool for committing and concealing theft. Mobile fraud teams move from one geographical area to another, or inflict wounds on victims from distant locations through telephones, by mail, and by advertisements. Insurance frauds, employing arson to generate profits, affect the safety and the health of our urban areas and their inhabitants. Looming on the horizon is the specter of the so-called cashless society, promising the possibility of fraudulent exploitation of systems created for the electronic transfer of funds. Faced with all this, prosecutors and policymakers who think beyond their immediate work tasks or their next day in court must ask fundamental questions about what they are doing and how they allocate financial and personnel resources to achieve their objectives. ''National strategy'' is simply a way of describing a hoped-for program that will make it possible to set priorities, to obtain the needed resources, and to allocate them where they can do the most good.

Notes

1. Edwin H. Sutherland, *White-Collar Crime* (New York: Dryden Press, 1949), p. 9.
2. Herbert Edelhertz, *The Nature, Impact, and Prosecution of White-Collar Crime,* U.S. Department of Justice, LEAA (Washington, D.C.: Government Printing Office, 1970), p. 3.
3. Hearings on White-Collar Crime before the Subcommittee on Crime of the Committee on the Judiciary, House of Representatives, 95th Cong., 2nd sess., 12 July 1978 (Washington, D.C.: Government Printing Office, 1979), p. 65.
4. U.S. Attorney General's First Annual Report on Federal Law Enforcement and Criminal Justice System Assistance Activities (Washington, D.C.: Government Printing Office, 1972), p. 161.
5. Edelhertz, *The Nature, Impact, and Prosecution,* note 2, p. 3. See also Walter C. Reckless, *The Crime Problem,* 4th ed. (New York: Appleton-Century-Crofts, 1978); Herbert Edelhertz, Ezra Stotland, Marilyn Walsh, and Milton Weinberg, *The Investigation of White-collar Crime* (Washington, D.C.: Government Printing Office, 1977), pp. 4–7.
6. Hearings on White-collar Crime, 12 July 1978, note 3, p. 69.

2 Symposium Background

Herbert Edelhertz and
Charles H. Rogovin

The National District Attorneys Association's (NDAA) Economic Crime Project commenced its operations in 1973 with 15 prosecutive units in Vermont, New York, Maryland, Florida, Texas, Kansas, Michigan, Ohio, Nebraska, California, and Washington. By 1978 it had expanded to 66 units in 34 states, with support services provided by a central staff located in Washington, D.C. In 1973 resources for this project were provided by the 15 offices themselves, and by the Law Enforcement Assistance Administration's (LEAA) Adjudication Division, a part of its Office of Criminal Justice Programs.

In 1978 the project reached a watershed. It was difficult to assess its impact in conventional evaluative terms because of the absence of baseline data and the absence of a consistent system for collection of information on all the project's activities. In addition, the number of units in the project had grown dramatically. Beyond this, however, it was also clear that there was no dependable way of measuring performance in a white-collar-crime prosecutive unit. One could not ground an assessment on the number of investigations or prosecutions undertaken or on a simple scorecard of victories versus defeats. Prosecuting and winning more cases might mean that a prosecutive unit had become more effective and successful; it might just as easily mean that the unit was taking on the easy cases and avoiding the hard ones. Consequently, assessments of success of failure rested more on "expert" opinion than on empirical data.

Nevertheless, certain results were evident by 1978. A clear recognition had developed, on the part of prosecutors in every part of the United States, that enforcement of laws against white-collar crime was the business of the local prosecutor as well as of federal prosecutors. Local prosecutors were more ready than ever before to commit resources of staff and dollars to this effort, even in the face of competing demands for resources to deal with violent crime and property crimes. Cadres of local assistant district attorneys had been trained and battle hardened and were moving beyond simple cases to take on more sophisticated fraud schemes including state antitrust offenses. Communication networks had developed among the assistant district attorneys staffing these economic crime units and some were coordinating actions across jurisdictional lines (sometimes across the continent). The units embarked on or strengthened a number of innovative approaches to protect the public; in many offices consumer-mediation services were

11

provided, and prosecutors exercised great creativity in invoking civil remedies on behalf of victims. The Economic Crime Project also established a clearinghouse in one of its participating units to deal with a particularly pernicious and widespread pattern of fraud, business opportunity schemes. The clearinghouse collected information on *modi operandi,* on fraud operators and their movements, and on investigative and prosecutive techniques and made it available to investigative and prosecutive agencies.

Notwithstanding its internal assessment of the worth of this effort, the leadership of the NDAA Economic Crime Committee ordered a review of its own performance, to determine whether it was doing the right things, whether it was doing them well, and—most important—whether there were things it should be doing that it was not. The committee wanted to know if there were improvements that could be made in both individual unit performance (in district attorneys' offices) and in the support services provided to the units by the Economic Crime Project Center. The Battelle Law and Justice Study Center was commissioned to undertake this review. The study center had been instrumental in the development of the Economic Crime Project and had provided policy planning and evaluative efforts for the project in 1973, 1974, and 1975. Now in 1978, more than two years later, it was returning to see what had happened in the interim and to assess the project's future.

The potential of the Economic Crime Project was first considered by an advisory panel that reviewed its past and current activities. This panel unanimously concluded that, just as white-collar offenders operate in disregard of local boundaries and in the face of federal, state, and local law-enforcement efforts, so the law-enforcement response must be rationally organized to meet the crime challenge such offenders present. It therefore concluded that there was a pressing need for development of a national strategy to deal with white-collar crime; one that would encompass the activities of federal, state, and local authorities, of prosecutors, investigative agencies, state attorneys general, and regulatory agencies. Based on this conclusion, the NDAA made the development of a national strategy to deal with white-collar crime a major element in its Economic Crime Project program. It determined that participation in implementation of such a strategy would be the responsibility of its units in prosecutors' offices as well as its national program leadership. This decision complemented developing plans in the U.S. Department of Justice, which had also identified the need for a national strategy and which was then considering options for the structure of such a program. Coordination of these two efforts was clearly in order.

It was comparatively easy to adopt national strategy development as a program objective, but more difficult to undertake and implement action to achieve this objective. Clearly, some way had to be found to improve mechanisms and techniques to coordinate investigations and prosecutions of white-collar-crime offenses that are subject to concurrent federal, state, and local jurisdiction. New sources of support had to be found to permit implementation of these mechanisms and use of these techniques. Special efforts would have to be undertaken to establish and to improve liaison among agencies at different jurisdictional levels, performing different functions. It would be necessary to define certain policy and operational issues including, but not limited to, those that involved resource allocation, mutual enforcement planning efforts, the identification of enforcement gaps and duplicative operations, and handling conflicts over "turf."

Conceiving a plan for a white-collar-crime-containment strategy required immediate consideration of several critical issues. First, that it is difficult to detect white-collar crime. The detection problem lies in the nature of both the crime and in the capabilities available for containment. The distinction between illicit and legal behavior is often unclear; the question is often not one of who did what, but whether the behavior in question was coextensive with the proscription of a technical statute and was committed with clearly provable intent. Over the years the level of law-enforcement concern about white-collar crime has been substantially lower than for other law-enforcement challenges. Therefore adequate resources for detection have not been available. For example, in this age of political and corporate corruption, people tolerate crimes such as cutting corners on taxes because "everyone does it" or because the violation does not resemble a street crime. Economic and political barriers are raised to discourage enforcement actions that may cause the public to question commercial and financial industry practices or that might undercut public and budgetary support for otherwise desirable welfare, benefit, and public-works programs.

The absence of well-thought-out containment strategies means that white-collar-crime offenders will be treated with undue lenience because there is no systematically gathered body of information on the impact of the crime on its victims or the community to counter the relative appeal of seemingly respectable defendants who use words rather than weapons to steal other people's money. It also means that there are inadequate remedies for victims and that existing laws will be enforced only in a sporadic fashion. With a multiplicity of alternative private and public administrative and regulatory remedies available for white-collar-type behavior, it sometimes appears inappropriate to enforce criminal sanctions, and these alternatives offer an easy way out of complex enforcement responsibilities.

Second, the scope and impact of white-collar crime are only dimly seen and felt. Dependence on unreliable, wide-ranging estimates of white-collar crime can result in a misdirected national containment strategy. Without fully understanding the nature and extent of white-collar crime, it is impossible to pinpoint the steps required to effectively mount a broad and effective white-collar-crime-control effort. For example, according priority to a white-collar-crime-control strategy that focuses on organizations that commit crimes against individuals may result in the exclusion of offenses committed by individuals. Individual crimes against social-welfare programs illustrate how a few crimes, taken one by one, may appear inconsequential but in total significantly erode government integrity and cripple confidence necessary for public support of such programs.

Third, as noted earlier, the mix of white-collar-crime-control responses is presently distributed among an array of agencies that offer administrative, civil, and criminal remedies. No one response is effective alone. Yet the present mix is not coherently organized to effectively challenge white-collar crime. Detection, investigation, and prosecution operate within legitimate constraints including legal jurisdiction, lack of resources, and inconsistent enforcement policies. There are numerous illustrations of policies operating at cross-purposes. For example, consumer protection is relatively uncoordinated on the federal level, with responsibilities located in various agencies and departments. It is even more fragmented in the state, local, and private sectors. Antitrust-enforcement responsibilities are divided between the Department of Justice, the Federal Trade Commission (FTC), state attorneys general, and local prosecutors. It is often mere chance that determines what agency, if any, responds to particular behavior and with what remedy. If white-collar crime is to be contained, careful consideration must be given to the allocation of presently limited resources among potentially active agencies.

Fourth, private and public responses to white-collar-crime control presently reveal serious gaps, as well as duplicative jurisdictional and organizational arrangements. Private businesses spend hundreds of millions of dollars every year on internal audits to detect and deter white-collar crime. The insurance industry, for example, mounts investigative programs specifically directed against white-collar crime. Unfortunately, the enforcement value of all these efforts is limited. Business is reluctant to refer cases for criminal prosecution because publicity could put the victimized company in a bad light, upset stockholders, or expose officers and directors to litigation in which they would be charged with negligent management of company affairs.

Aside from the interaction between government and private industry, cooperation within government needs improvement. White-collar crime is often not adequately contained because there is little coordination between governmental agencies. Although the federal government has broad jurisdictional capability to cope with white-collar crime and a large albeit insufficient body of resources, local jurisdictions rarely have even a small part of the technical, investigative, or prosecutive manpower that they need. Vigorous measures to clarify and rationalize relationships and resource allocations between governmental levels is clearly required.

The timing of the NDAA initiative, in the nonfederal portion of the effort, to develop a national strategy to deal with white-collar crime was advantageous. In the months preceding this decision the Department of Justice designated the battle against white-collar crime as one of its major priorities. Then-Attorney General Griffin B. Bell and then-Deputy Attorney General Benjamin R. Civiletti expressed their determination to develop such a national strategy. At the same time plans were being made by the Subcommittee on Crime of the House Committee on the Judiciary to launch a series of hearings to examine the character and impact of white-collar crime in the United States, to look at the nature of federal and other responses to such crime, and to determine whether adequate efforts and resources were being devoted to containment of white-collar crime. The subcommittee was also planning specifically to address the need for some coordinated national program to deal with white-collar crime.

The symposium that is the central subject of this book was the core of the NDAA Economic Crime Project effort to contribute to the development of this national strategy. It was designed to surface the relevant and critical issues. What are the agencies and who are the parties, in the private as well as the public sector, who should be included in such an effort? What are the barriers to the development of a national strategy, and to its implementation? At this symposium, which was held at the Battelle Conference Center in Seattle, Washington, on 20–21 July 1978, these issues were discussed as part of a carefully structured agenda by a panel consisting of local prosecutors, representatives of the FBI, the Criminal Division of the Department of Justice, the SEC, the LEAA, the American Bar Association (ABA), a state attorney general's office, and various representatives from adademia, research institutes, a congressional subcommittee, the judiciary, and the private sector. (See appendix A for a list of participants and issues discussed.) The symposium was cochaired by the editors of this volume: Herbert Edelhertz, Director of the Battelle Law and Justice Study Center, and Professor Charles H. Rogovin, Temple University Law School.

As reflected in parts II, III, and IV of this volume, the symposium was designed to address the critical issues involved in the development of a national strategy by dividing the subject into three broad topics. A paper was commissioned that would address each of the three topics and provide the basis for discussion by the expert panel that had been assembled. Each of these discussions in turn was the subject of a rapporteurial paper prepared by the Battelle staff. The panel members were the principal sources of expertise on white-collar crime in the symposium. In order to bring new insights to bear on the task of developing a national strategy and to avoid many of the limitations that are inherent in reliance on experts with a particular interest or focus, discussion papers were sought from authors who could offer fresh and thought-provoking contributions to the design, development, and implementation of a national strategy to deal with white-collar crime, and not from those who had special credentials in the field of white-collar-crime research and enforcement.

Part II of this book consists of a paper presented and discussed by Professor Mark Moore of Harvard University's John F. Kennedy School of Government. Its subject is "White-collar Crime as Fraud, Abuses of Organizational Malfeasance: A Preliminary Analysis." Dr. Marilyn E. Walsh of the Battelle staff then comments on the ensuing symposium discussion of the institutional challenge of white-collar-crime problem and the implications for institutions and institutional arrangements are considered. Exploration of the barriers to, as well as the potential for, the interaction of such institutions with the criminal-justice system are examined to identify key elements needed for a coherent white-collar-crime containment effort.

In part III Daniel L. Skoler of the ABA considers white-collar-crime containment in the context of our nation's criminal-justice system. Dr. Mary V. McGuire of the Battelle staff then comments on the panel's response to the Skoler paper. The thrust of this discussion was that white-collar-crime control requires more than the criminal-justice system can alone provide. Yet strategies to control white-collar crime necessarily place special pressures on and generate competition for limited resources in a system that currently has difficulty controlling street crime. Specialized requirements of white-collar-crime containment complicate the criminal-justice system's pursuit of its goals in prevention, detection, investigation, and prosecution of common, non-white-collar crime. Therefore consideration must be given to how to effectively develop, marshal, and distribute resources for white-collar-crime containment in the face of such strains and competition.

In part IV, William Morrill of Mathematica Policy Research considers how a national strategy can be developed and implemented. The discussion that followed is described and analyzed by Frederic A. Morris of the Battelle staff. Part IV also includes an examination of the issues and insights that are involved in developing a national white-collar-crime-containment strategy. Problems are highlighted to explain the trade-offs and the wide range of policy alternatives that must be considered. Included is an example that considers the implications of the criminal-justice system's assuming exclusive responsibility for white-collar-crime control.

Parts II, III, and IV can be considered together as part of a sequence that starts with the question of the challenge to be dealt with by a national strategy to contain white-collar crime. It goes on in part III to consider the place of enforcement against white-collar crime as part of our criminal-justice system since the shape of any such national strategy must be influenced by existing realities, and enforcement efforts must go forward under essentially current conditions while a national strategy is being designed and implemented. This leads naturally to part IV, which considers how we can go about the development of such a strategy.

Chapter 9 and the appendixes are a review of the developmental efforts that followed this symposium and that were influenced by it. It is fair to state that a philosophy emerged from this symposium that substantially influenced the directions and activities of the NDAA Economic Crime Project National Strategy Program in the many months of effort that followed the Seattle symposium of July 1978.

**Part II
The Nature of the
White-Collar-Crime Problem**

3 Notes toward a National Strategy to Deal with White-Collar Crime

Mark H. Moore

The Problem of Defining White-Collar Crime

Despite serious attention, a suitable definition of "white-collar crime" has remained problematic. At least two separate traditions exist. One tradition focuses on economic crimes: fraud, bunko schemes, embezzlement, stock manipulations, insurance fraud, and general chiseling in economic transactions. The common characteristics of these offenses are that they depend on deception within the institutions (and among the exchanges) of the private economy, and inflict financial (rather than physical) losses on their victims. The usual justification for paying attention to such offenses is that the total economic losses associated with such offenses are large enough (relative to losses suffered in street crimes such as robberies, burglaries, and larcenies) to warrant priority attention in deploying enforcement resources.

A second somewhat older tradition suggests a broader concept—that individuals who hold powerful institutional positions in the society can victimize others in ways that are every bit as costly and offensive as the acts of street criminals but escape punishment either by hiding their offenses within complex institutional processes or by relying on their apparent respectability to ward off investigation, prosecution, and sentencing. The original focus of this older tradition was on the same offenses that now preoccupy those concerned with economic crime, for example, fraud and embezzlement. But while the offenses were the same, the features of the offenses that motivated the interest of the older tradition were quite different. The older tradition was less interested in the size of the economic losses to victims than the irony that an individual in an established position in the society could steal sums that made the "take" in ordinary street crimes seem ridiculously small, but face much lower risks of punishment than street criminals. This simple irony highlighted two facts to which they wished to draw attention: (1) the existence of substantial institutional power in the society; and (2) the inevitable unfairness of the criminal-justice system as it confronted the power of privileged positions. These observations in turn tapped powerful ideological themes in the U.S. society, (for example, a fundamental fear of institutional power and thoroughgoing desire for equality before the law) and motivated an attack on white-collar crime.

21

In the context of recent history, these broad themes of institutional power and unfairness in the criminal-justice system have become even more potent than they were forty years ago. We see all around us evidence of the capacity of large institutions to exploit and injure ordinary citizens and to resist even the most determined regulatory efforts. Thus in the modern context these broad themes defining white-collar crime naturally embrace offenses such as price fixing, willful violations of environmental and safety regulations, the production and marketing of dangerous or shoddy merchandise, illegal campaign contributions to maintain favorable tax rulings, and so on, as well as large-scale stealing. Moreover, once one includes abuses of private corporate power in his definition of white-collar crime, it is hard to justify the exclusion of abuses of governmental and political power as well. Thus illegal wiretapping by government agencies, election fraud managed by dominant political parties, and the solicitation of bribes or other favors by government officials might all be included in the definition of white-collar crime. The common element of all these offenses is that they are committed with relative impunity by people in powerful institutional positions—sometimes for their own purposes and sometimes to further the interests of their institutions.

Clearly, there are significant differences between these two definitions of white-collar crime. One emphasizes economic gains to individuals as a result of deception or abuses of trust. The other emphasizes the power of institutions (and individuals in institutional positions) to victimize others and successfully resist criminal prosecution. While there are significant overlaps, the wide divergence in their respective orientations is striking.

Of course, we could treat the problem of defining white-collar crime with impatience—a matter of mere semantics, far divorced from pressing substantive choices about the design of a national strategy. My own view, however, is that the definition of the problem is of the essence. How we think about the problem will at least partly determine our response—both the relative importance we attach to it and the particular way we decide to deploy our resources.

In fact, there is a special temptation in talking about white-collar crime. As we have seen, the concept is capable of sustaining a broad definition that taps fundamental ideological themes and widespread concerns. As such, the concept is potent in mobilizing and sustaining a broad and interested constituency. On the other hand, when it comes to designing specific programs, the broad concept becomes too diffuse. Even worse, it seems to point us toward objectives that we know will be extremely difficult to accomplish. Hence when we turn to designing specific programs to deal with white-collar crime, we tend to adopt a narrower definition more consistent with our current institutional inclinations and capabilities. This situation tempts us into committing a kind of "policy fraud." We use the broad definition of the problem when we want to attract interest, authority and resources, and we use the narrower definition when we plan programmatic action. The predictable result is disillusionment among those who lent their support to a broad objective only to discover that the actual programmatic activity occurs along a narrower and less important front. Of course, by this time we may all be relatively inured to "policy fraud." But one might expect a group of people concerned about white-collar crime to be more chary than most about promising effective action in a broader area than they can in fact achieve.

At the outset then we probably owe it to the constituency we expect to be concerned about white-collar crime to define the problem in a way that reliably captures their major substantive and symbolic concerns. We should resist the temptation to define the problem in a way that is merely convenient or consistent with emergent institutional interests and capabilities. If after having looked at the broader social concerns at stake in this area, we decide that we want to define the problem more narrowly or more pragmatically, that will be fine. We will tend at least be in a position to describe what has been left out and why. And we will not be guilty of deluding ourselves about how much of what might be considered white-collar crime is in fact being addressed by our policies.

A Broad Perspective on White-Collar Crime

As individual citizens pursuing the good life, we seek to protect our property, health, freedom, and sense of security against a variety of external threats—some from natural forces and some from human agencies. To control some of the potential threats from human agencies, we pass laws prohibiting certain acts under penalty of criminal sanctions. In doing so, we immediately enhance the citizen's sense of security by allowing him to have expectations that he will *ordinarily* be free from the threats represented by the prohibited acts. As a corollary, we also entitle the citizen to feel victimized when a human agency injures him by an act that is prohibited by law and to call on the government for help in recouping his losses and restoring his sense of security.

Of course, existing laws invoking criminal sanctions fall way short of protecting us from all threats under human control. We can still fail to be hired, lose our job, buy shoddy merchandise, or be injured in an automobile accident without any crime's having been committed. Moreover, even in areas where we are protected by the existence of laws and the availability of publicly provided enforcement resources, we still quite naturally expect to shoulder a large share of the burden of defending ourselves. At the very least, we are expected to complain to enforcement agencies when we have been victimized and to assist them in their investigative and prosecution efforts. More often we assume responsibility for resisting our own victimization through some combination of vigilence, caution, and vigorous self-defense. Still in a variety of areas we feel entitled to expect government protection and to feel victimized when that protection fails.

Historically our laws and enforcement efforts have been designed primarily to protect us from physical attacks and thefts by other individuals in the society. We have acted as if the capacity of other individuals to threaten us physically or to steal our possessions when we were not looking were the most significant *human* threats to our individual sense of well-being. To a great extent our continued preoccupation with street crime is a legacy of this common-law tradition—now buttressed by the existence of professional police forces who are organized primarily to protect us from these kinds of offenses and offenders.

Recently, however, we seem to have recognized that our property, health, freedom, and sense of security are vulnerable to methods other than physical attack and surreptitious entry, and to offenders who differ from violent or stealthy individuals. Specifically, we have noticed that we are vulnerable through deception and exploitation of an unequal bargaining position as well as through physical attack and stealth. Moreover, we sense that the increasing complexity of the society and the emergence of large institutions with discretionary control over valued opportunities have dramatically increased our vulnerability to both deception and exploitation. Partly in response to these new, real dangers and partly in response to increased demands for government protection in areas where we used to rely only on vigorous self-defense, we have passed laws (many with criminal sanctions attached) that are targeted on these ''new'' offenses and offenders. It is this nexus of subtle but potent mechanisms of victimizing others, changes in social conditions that have allowed these mechanisms to come into play more often, and increased demands for governmental control that has yielded a substantial white-collar-crime problem. The relationships are sufficiently complex and important to merit some elaboration.

Characteristic Modes of Victimization of White-Collar Crime

Reflection reveals remarkably few mechanisms to take from a person something that he values and has a right to have. The obvious methods are those characteristic of steet crime: stealth or physical attack. Both methods allow an aggressive offender to extract something he values from a surprised and reluctant victim. The victim suffers not only material and physical losses but also such psychological losses as shame for his inability to defend himself and a heightened sense of his vulnerability to similar attacks in the future.

Beyond these measures typical of street crime, two other methods exist that seem characteristic of white-collar crimes. One of these is deception. A person gives up something of value in exchange for something he has been led to believe will be of roughly equivalent value and finds that the thing he receives is worth much less—perhaps nothing at all. This is the classic definition of a *fraud*.

A second method of victimization characteristic of white-collar offenses resembles extortion but does not depend on a threat of physical force. It occurs when an offender has discretionary control over some resource or opportunity whose disposition is of enormous importance to the victim and a matter of relative indifference to the offender. Moreover, there is some rule or expectation governing the disposition of the valued resource or opportunity (known to both offender and victim) that would entitle the victim to his preferred disposition. Instead of simply making the preferred disposition on the appropriate terms, however, the offender insists on some special remuneration. Depending on the value of the resource or opportunity to the victim, and the strength of the victim's claim on the resource even without the special contribution, the amount extorted by the offender and the sensation of victimization may be more or less severe. This is the classic case of *exploitation,* that is, one person's exacting maximum advantage from an unequal bargaining position, despite the fact that the terms of the exchange were supposed to have been set in advance.

These methods of victimization are characteristic of white-collar offenses for two different reasons. First, they occur among the exchanges and social interactions that are part and parcel of our daily lives. There is nothing exotic or strange about the events surrounding the offenses. There is no trespass and no attack. It is only the outcomes that are unexpected and unpleasant. In fact, the offenses probably could not occur without exchange systems that for the most part were reliable and fair. Second, to be successful, the offender must either appear to or actually occupy some relatively powerful institutional position within the society. Deception works best if the offender can surround himself with the credentials and trappings that make him part of our ordinary exchange economy. He must have "bonafides." An institutional position is even more obviously necessary in the case of exploitation. It is precisely the individual control over the substantial resources and opportunities that large institutions have to distribute that provides the representatives such enormous bargaining power. Thus these methods of victimization depend crucially on the existence of an organized society and the existence of institutional positions that can be occupied, or appear to be occupied, by individual offenders.

Note also that while the *methods* of victimization differ from those used in street crimes, the subjective experience of victimization may be quite similar. The victim can take either physical or economic losses—though economic losses are probably much more common. In addition, the victim may experience the same embarrassing sense of impotence and the same anxieties about his vulnerability to similar offenses in the future. In fact, in the case of exploitation, the sense of degradation and anxiety about the future are likely to be particularly intense. There may be nothing the victim can do to alter the conditions that originally led to his victimization: He may continue to need whatever the institution (or its representative) has to offer; if so, the institution may continue to get from him more than he expected to pay. Since there seems to be no way out for the victim, the sense of powerlessness may be particularly acute. Thus while methods of white-collar victimization may seem subtler and less direct than the methods of street crime, they are equally cruel.

Social Conditions Creating Greater Scope for
White-Collar Crimes

Of course, these methods of victimization have always been available to potential offenders. It is likely, however, that recent changes in both the organization of the society and our determination to control the behavior of people within large institutions have vastly increased the extent of what is now perceived to be the white-collar-crime problem.

One significant change is the continuing elaboration of the network of exchange relationships in which individuals find themselves enmeshed. It used to be true that important economic transactions were conducted primarily either within a family or between the family and a small number of institutions. The transactions were relatively few, relatively simple so that neither side had a great deal more information about the exchange than the other, and conducted by individuals who expected to have long-term relationships so that neither side would be willing to risk their relationship for a small advantage in a given exchange. Now, partly as the result of a continuing process of differentiation and specialization that occurs with the growth of an exchange economy, partly as the result of increased wealth that allows us to buy more complicated products, and partly as the result of a vast expansion of governmental activities paralleling the growth of the market economy, individuals find themselves dealing episodically in complex transactions with many different institutions. Moreover, many of these transactions are based implicitly or explicitly on trust because one party controls much of the relevant information on which the transaction is based. An auto mechanic knows more about what he did to a car than a customer can easily discover. The owner of a building may know more about its real worth than an insurance company. A welfare client knows more about her qualifying characteristics than the case worker. And a fire inspector may know more about the fire regulations governing the grant of a license to a restaurant owner than the owner does. Thus the sheer number and complexity of the transactions conspire with the absence of an expectation of a continuing relationship to create enormous opportunities for fraud and exploitation.

Note that opportunities for fraud and exploitation exist on both the supplier and the consumer or client side of the transaction. On the supplier side one hears of real-estate frauds, storm-window and aluminum-siding frauds, shoddy and fraudulent auto repairs, deceptive advertising and credit practices, and so on. On the consumer or client side, one can imagine forged checks, filing false insurance claims, income-tax evasion, and giving false information about eligibility for unemployment compensation. These are all examples of people's taking advantage of the looseness of their institutional relationships and the confusion marking their economic relationship to extract an advantage from their partner in the transaction. In sum, since we make many more transactions; since the transactions involve complex products, services, licenses and duties that are hard for both parties to the transaction to understand and verify; and since long-term reciprocal relationships have been shattered by the complexity and specialization of the society; the capacity of agents on either side of the transaction to police the transactions and defend their interests has been reduced. Since it is hard to know what is happening in the transaction and few incentives to resist the temptation to take advantage, many people will be tempted to exploit the ignorance.

A second significant change related to but different from the elaboration of the exchange economy is the emergence of large institutions with discretionary control over resources and activities that are valuable (perhaps even vital) to other individuals. The emergence of these large institutions affects the opportunities to commit white-collar offenses in three important and different ways.

First, these institutions lend credibility and distribute authority among individual representatives. In doing so, they increase the opportunities for the *individuals* who represent the institutions to deceive and exploit other individuals who do business with or have an interest in the activities of the institution. An auto repairman working for a nationally recognized company can get away with a shoddy repair job more easily than an unaffiliated mechanic by hiding behind his organizational affiliation. A welfare case worker may get away with underestimating the benefits for which an applicant is eligible by virtue of his official position and apparent expertise. Similarly, hiring and contracting officials in both public and private agencies may abuse their discretionary authority over these crucial decisions by extracting special favors from people or firms who could reasonably expect to be chosen by merit alone. And government officials with the discretionary authority to distribute a subsidy, grant a privilege, or enforce a costly obligation may "extort" some payment or service from individuals even when the citizens have a clear right (under current policies) to receive the subsidy, be granted the privilege, or escape the obligation. As the reach of these insitutions has grown, so have the opportunities of people who represent them to deceive and exploit other individuals who do business with them.

Second, the institutions have become relatively vulnerable *victims* of white-collar offenses as well as potential offenders. The reason is simply that the institutions distribute control over their resources and influence over their operations and policies to a large number of individuals who man positions throughout the organization. These insiders may take advantage of their position to steal the organization's assets, depart from an operational policy in exchange for a fee from outsiders who have an interest in changing current policies, or simply sell inside information about the organization's plans, interests, or capabilities. Thus bank tellers embezzle money, payroll clerks collude with line supervisors to create false payroll records, contracting officers arrange for kickbacks in making procurement decisions, real-estate owners collude with government housing officials to guarantee a mortgage that is far above the real value of a property, and high government officials promise to "do what they can" for companies that have tax, antitrust, or regulatory problems. These cases differ from the preceding ones in that it is the institution itself that is victimized by its own employees and agents, not its clients or customers.

Third, the institutions can become offenders themselves. Or, somewhat more precisely, the institutions can motivate their representatives to take actions that serve the interests of the organizations (and may even have been implicitly or explicitly authorized by higher-level officials) but are also in violation of criminal statutes. This situation has developed because we have decided to regulate the conduct of many of our institutions and have relied (at least partly) on criminal sanctions to do so.

Now part of our determination to regulate these institutions comes simply from a recognition that the institutions sometimes have interests that differ from those of the society at large. Moreover, their pursuit of their interests may injure the rest of us. Among economic institutions, the pursuit of profits may lead to production processes that are dirtier or more dangerous than they need be or to efforts to fix prices substantially above levels to which they would be driven if free competition were allowed to prevail. Among governmental institutions, an enforcement agency's interest in making cases, a regulatory agency's interest in reaching an accommodation with a powerful, regulated industry, or a political party's interest in retaining local power may lead to decisions and actions that inflict substantial losses on the rest of us.

A second part of our motivation to regulate the institutions, however, springs from a recognition that since these institutions incorporate and organize much of the society's activity, we have no choice but to turn to them when we want to accomplish large public purposes. Thus to affect the supply of suitable jobs, we pass minimum-wage laws; to guarantee income to retired workers, we insist on minimum standards for pension plans; to guarantee equality of educational opportunity, we require the integration of public schools; and to reduce discrimination throughout the society, we mandate affirmative-action plans. In all these cases we are drawn to the regulation of major institutions not because of their capacity to do harm if left alone but simply because they are the actors who have the capacity to help us with broad social goals.

The motivation to regulate the conduct of large institutions does not always result in the passage of statutes with criminal sanction for noncompliance. We are apt to rely more frequently on the mechanisms of private civil suits and regulatory agencies that set rules and enforce compliance through civil sanctions than on criminal statutes and criminal prosecution. Still in a surprising (and growing) number of areas, we have been willing to establish criminal sanctions to buttress the mechanisms of civil suits and governmental regulatory action. As a result, major officials, acting on behalf of large institutions (even with their explicit authorization), are exposed to criminal liability.

The net effect of all this is to produce a society in which the opportunities for individuals to commit white-collar offenses have increased dramatically. Part of the increase reflects changes in the operation of society that hold real dangers of victimization. Part reflects an increase in our demand for government assistance in defending our interests. And part reflects an increased determination to control the behavior of large institutions that have significant potential for good and ill. The combination leads to a potentially vast agenda for enforcement programs against white-collar offenses.

The Insistent Demand for Equal Justice

Arrayed against this vast agenda is a very small criminal-justice system currently overwhelmed and preoccupied by the problem of street crime. Given the disappointments and frustrations of our current efforts to deal with street crime, one is tempted to counsel against requiring the criminal-justice system to take on any new burdens, particularly one as large and knotty as white-collar crime. But it is precisely our current desperate efforts to deal with street crime that make it seem unusually important that we do something about white-collar crime as well. It is clear that we fear street crime. Moreover, in recent years we have become less sanguine about the prospects of dealing with this problem through the rehabilitation of offenders. Hence we are increasingly inclined to crack down on muggers, armed robbers, rapists, murderers, and burglars. The commitment to harshness in handling street criminals combines with a traditional ideologic commitment to fairness in the criminal-justice system to make the issue of the criminal-justice system's response to white-collar crime of acute importance. We admit the possibility of significant victimization through methods and offenders that look much different than ordinary street offenses. In fact, we have already established criminal sanctions for some of the offenses. So fairness requires us to strike out at white-collar offenders as well as street criminals. In fact, given the intensity of our attack on street crime, there seems to be a *special* obligation to prosecute respectable people who use their position and reputation to steal through deception and exploitation. Until such attacks are visible, we worry about the fundamental fairness and rationality of the criminal-justice system.

Summary

In sum, in my view, rather fundamental symbolic and substantive issues are evoked by the concept of "white-collar crime." We are as worried about stealing and hurting and frightening people when it is done through deception and exploitation by people who occupy institutional positions (or, indeed, by the institutions themselves), as when it is done by people who rely on stealth and physical assaults. In fact, we are particularly worried when these acts are done on a wholesale basis by institutions that simply ignore the legal obligations that are supposed to restrain them. Moreover, throughout the entire area, we are concerned about fairness in the criminal-justice system. We think it is outrageous that people with institutional positions would find it relatively easy to steal large sums of money with impunity. And we want to be reassured that we are as eager to prosecute powerful people who commit crimes on behalf of their institutions as well as relatively poor people who commit crimes for themselves. In my view, it is in terms of these broad issues that we must design and evaluate any national strategy to respond to the problem of white-collar crime.

Distinct Components of the White-Collar-Crime Problem

Anybody who has a vivid sense of the limited capabilities of the criminal-justice system and who has followed the argument this far should by now be shaking his head with worry. Arrayed against the vast agenda of white-collar offenses, the criminal-justice system seems too small, too clumsy, and too fragile. It is inconceivable that the criminal-justice system could deal with any substantial portion of the individual incidents of fraud, embezzlement, graft, and abuses of authority that could occur in a society as large and complex and as wedded to the principle of *cavant emptor* as ours. Part of the problem is the sheer number of offenses that are likely to occur. But another part of the problem arises from the enormous expense of preparing cases of this type for prosecution.

Moreover, while we like to think that we are a government of laws and not men, one does not need too much experience with the actual operations of the criminal-justice system to understand that the men who work that system face acute personal dilemmas and risks in attacking institutions that represent significant economic, governmental, or political power. In enforcing environmental laws against a firm that threatens to close down if they are prosecuted, the criminal-justice official feels that he is dealing with a larger policy choice than he would like to deal with. Similarly, in attacking governmental and political institutions, the officials often feel they are attacking their peers and that their own motives will inevitably be suspect. The blade of the criminal law is simply apt to shatter when it is brought into contact with powerful political and economic institutions.

I am inclined to agree with this assessment and to worry that the criminal-justice system has bitten off much more than it can chew in taking on white-collar crime. But I would like to emphasize that we are already in this mess. We have already distributed criminal liability rather liberally among the activities and personnel of major social institutions. We have done so because we wanted to check the power we saw in those institutions and grasped the criminal law as one of society's mightiest weapons. Having created criminal liability, fairness forces us to enforce the laws. It is only then that we find that the criminal-justice system is more like a frail reed than a mighty whip.

So it is hard to decide to do nothing or to begin cutting back the use of criminal sanctions. We are impelled forward by the trends just described. In moving forward, however, we can already see that we will have to be guided by several major strategic principles. First, we should attack the problem of white-collar crime on a front that is broad enough to capture the major substantive and symbolic concerns evoked by the concept but narrow enough to be within the capabilities of the criminal-justice system. Second, we should organize our response to the substantive problem in a way that invites assistance from institutions other than the criminal-justice system and generally protects the criminal-justice system from either a significant overload or obvious unfairness. In the end we are likely to discover that the criminal-justice system plays a relatively minor role in a national strategy to control white-collar crime and that its role will be to punctuate or complement the actions of other institutions rather than bear the brunt of the main offensive.

A useful start in thinking operationally about a national strategy toward white-collar crime is to divide the problem into several distinct components. To be useful, the components should be defined in a way that allows us to make rough estimates about their relative importance and to make some broad judgments about how the problem can be approached—both by the criminal-justice system itself and by actors from outside the criminal-justice system. Based on reflection and discussion, it seems useful to divide the problem of white-collar crime into seven major components. Table 3–1 describes the basic characteristics of the different components. Each component will be discussed in greater detail as follows.

"Stings and Swindles"

The Nature of the Offense. The first component can be described as the problem of "stings and swindles." This component involves stealing through deception by individuals (or "rings") who have no continuing institutional position and whose major purpose from the outset is to bilk people of their money. The cons and frauds that are included within this category vary in size and in targets. At one extreme is an offender who makes a few fraudulent door-to-door sales of pans, encyclopedias, or burial insurance. At another extreme are relatively sophisticated stock swindles where worthless or forged stock certificates are sold to large financial institutions. This category might even include large counterfeiting operations. What ties these varied offenses together is that individuals and institutions are tricked into giving up money to individuals who had no intention other than stealing and who are likely to disappear once the deception is successfully accomplished.

For purposes of both gauging the relative seriousness of the problem and thinking of effective responses, it is useful to compare this offense to burglary. The experience of victimization is similar. Losses are economic rather than physical. And while the victim is apt to feel humiliated by the fact that he was deceived, he is not likely to have the same sensations of trespass and anxiety about the future that a victim of burglary would. In gauging the seriousness of any given offense like this, then, we are likely to look at the total amount that was stolen, the capacity of the victims to absorb the loss, and the relative innocence and frailness of the victim. We are likely to feel angrier about a man who bilks ten to twenty elderly poor for $500 a piece in a burial-insurance fraud than a second offender who sells fake stock certificates alleged to be "hot" to a shady stock broker for $50,000. We would analyze the social cost of specific burglaries in about the same terms. While the social costs of these offenses in aggregate are not clear, I would be surprised if the problem of stings and swindles turned out to be more serious than that of burglary.

Control Possibilities. The analogy with burglary also helps in thinking about effective responses. A little reflection suggests that while we are fundamentally dependent on potential victims to prevent burglaries by locking doors and guarding property, we will be even more dependent on self-

Table 3-1
General Characteristics of Different Components of White-Collar Crime

Component of White-Collar Crime	Defining Characteristics				Agencies Involved		
	Nature of Offender	Nature of Victim	Mode of Victimization	Losses	Detecting	Prosecuting	Punishing
"Stings and Swindles"	Noninstitutional position: individuals or "rings"	Individuals and organizations	Deception	Primarily economic	Primarily victims	Primarily CJS	Primarily CJS
"Chiseling"	Individuals with institutional positions	Clients or consumers of institution	Deception	Primarily economic	Institution (?) victims (?)	Primarily institutions	Primarily institutions
"Individual abuses of institutional position"	Individuals with institutional positions	Clients or consumers of institution	Exploitation	Primarily economic but also psychological	Institutions; victims	Primarily institutions	Primarily institutions
Embezzlement and employer fraud	Individuals with institutional positions	Institution itself	Deception	Distributed economic losses	Exclusively institutions	Primarily institutions	Primarily institutions
Client fraud	Clients of financial institutions	Institution itself	Deception	Distributed economic losses	Exclusively institutions	Primarily institutions	
Influence peddling/ bribery	Individuals with institutional positions	Institution itself	Collusion between outsiders and insiders	Primarily economic	Victims (?) institutions (?)	Institutions (?) CJS (?)	Institutions (?) CJS (?)
Willful institutional noncompliance	Institutions themselves	Society at large	Exploitation of bargaining position	Economic; physical; psychological	Regulatory agencies	Regulatory agencies	Regulatory agencies

defense in preventing cons. After all, burglaries produce a few signs that are potentially visible to patrolling police. Stings and swindles do not. Hence the victims will be much more on their own in defending against offenders. Once the offense has been committed, though, it may be easier to identify and prosecute the offender in a con game than in a burglary. The reason is simply that the victim is likely to have seen and come to know a little about the offender. The major obstacle to successful detection and prosecution may be nothing more than a limited jurisdiction that is easily escaped by the offender. Thus, as in handling burglaries, an effective response to stings and swindles will depend a great deal on individual self-defense and the willingness of victims to submit complaints and assist in the investigation. The criminal-justice role is likely to be nothing more than deciding how serious a complaint is and how many resources to devote to the investigation. No opportunity for a more aggressive or pro-active enforcement strategy seems immediately available.

"Chiseling"

The Nature of the Offense. The second component of the problem is "chiseling," that is, giving a customer or client less than he has a right to expect on the basis of an institution's announced policies. This component resembles the offenses above in that it involves stealing (on an ad-hoc basis) through deception. It differs from the last category in that the offenders are people who occupy continuing institutional positions, and the deception is not complete. In effect, somebody who expects to be in business for a while decides on an ad-hoc basis to supply "half a loaf." Typical offenses are auto-repair frauds, "short-weighting" in supermarkets and gas stations, or refusing to grant some privilege or provide some service that a client is entitled to in a government bureaucracy. The offender is usually an individual employee (or a relatively small unit of a much larger organization) who decides to cheat on an obligation to customers, clients, or another firm by doing something that is contrary to his institution's policies but that saves him some trouble or earns him a small, nonorganizationally provided, reward.

Altogether, the victimization associated with these offenses can be quite large. For example, it has been estimated that the public loses more than $20 billion each year in auto-repair frauds. But even so, the experience of the individual victims may not be all that serious. For the most part, the loss will be nothing more than a relatively small economic loss. There will be few physical consequences. And the experience of humiliation and fear (with its lasting effects on one's general sense of security) may not occur at all. In fact, the victim may not even notice that he has been victimized. So while economic losses to victims in offenses like this may be large in total, the individual experience of victimization may be sufficiently different to make these offenses much less important than other kinds of offenses that inflict fewer total losses but do so by inflicting very large economic, physical, and psychological losses on a few unsuspecting victims.

Control Possibilities. The fact that the victims may not even notice that they have been victimized creates a major problem in controlling the offenses. There is no one to resist the offenses or to identify the offenders. (This is probably the main reason that the total losses can get so large.) Still, in trying to control offenses of this kind, the criminal-justice system does have a crucial ally—the institutions themselves. To the extent that the institutions have quality-control policies that are important for them to follow (for either marketing or legal reasons), they will make enormous efforts to "police" their own employee's conduct. In doing so, they will, of course, prevent some of the possible offenses in this category. Similarly, to the extent that trade associations and professional associations exist to protect the reputation of their particular service or industry, they might be enlisted in efforts to control chiseling. Of course, these associations have much smaller capacities to detect and deal with specific instances of chiseling, but it would be an error to ignore their possible contribution.

Since institutions and professional associations have some capacity to prevent chiseling and since much of the chiseling that does occur will either go unnoticed (or be handled informally in complaints by clients and consumers to the institutions and associations), it is probably safe to say that only a tiny piece of this problem will ever end up in the lap of the government and even less in the formal machinery of the criminal-justice system. The government becomes involved primarily through two kinds of agencies: licensing boards that are designed to guarantee quality in the provision of certain kinds of services and (more recently) consumer-advocacy organizations that are set up to receive and process complaints from consumers. Usually these agencies have only civil powers. The criminal-justice system becomes involved only when these regulatory agencies want to press criminal cases, or where state attorneys general or local district attorneys have set up aggressive consumer-protection bureaus designed to make criminal cases against merchants who bilk the public.

If one wanted to increase the level of government effort in this area, the right strategy would probably involve some combination of: (1) increasing the volume of complaints made to the government by widely advertising the rights of consumers and establishing a convenient procedure for lodging the complaint; and (2) some proactive investigations of firms, bureaus, or industries that seem to generate a large volume of complaints. In setting up such a system, however, the government would, in fact, be going after institutions that *systematically* violated clear obligations rather than going after the occasional, ad-hoc chiseler. Ad-hoc chiseling, as defined in this section, is probably beyond the reach of anyone but the institutions who employ the chiselers.

Individual Exploitation of Institutional Position

The Nature of the Offense. A third component of the white-collar-crime problem involves an individual's exploiting the power of an institutional position that confers control over valued privileges or resources to take advantage of another individual who has strong interest in how that power gets used. Typical offenses include a personnel officer in government or industry who extorts a kickback from a potential employee for a favorable hiring decision or a fire inspector who demands a payment from the owner of a restaurant to grant him a license.

In actual cases, it may be difficult to distinguish these abuses of institutional power from "bribery," to be discussed later. Analytically, however, the difference is quite clear. In offenses involving exploitation of institutional position, the victim has a clear right to something the official controls, and the official asks for an additional payment to make the required decision. The individual confronting the institution is the victim. The representative of the institution is the offender. In cases involving bribery, the situation is reversed. The individual confronting the institutional representative would *not* ordinarily be entitled to favorable treatment. In this situation it is the organization that is the victim. Both the representative and the outsider profit from the offense.

Note that the experience of victimization is likely to be much different for exploitation of institutional position than for other offenses discussed so far. The reason is simply that power rather than deception is the vehicle used to victimize. An individual with significant power confronts another individual with less power and forces him to accept less (or pay more) than he has a right to expect. Because power is being used, the experience of victims is likely to be quite different. They could experience physical abuse and humiliation as well as economic losses. Moreover, it is likely that the long-term effects on the victim's sense of security will be devastating. Encountering power ruthlessly used to exploit a victim is a much different experience than simply being tricked or deceived.

Control Possibilities. In thinking about an effective response to such offenses, one quickly sees that they will be much easier to handle than chiseling. We have the same important ally—namely, the institutions themselves who are likely to have some interest and capability for detecting and punishing the offenses. In addition, we are likely to get more help from victims who are more likely to notice that they have been victimized and to be indignant about their victimization. As a result, many of these cases will be handled administratively within the organizations whose representatives have exploited their positions. The general strategy to improve enforcement against such offenses would resemble the strategy against chiseling: (1) widespread advertising of rights and the establishment of a convenient complaint procedure; and (2) some proactive undercover operations by criminal-justice agencies in areas where one expects to see a great deal of "official extortion."

Note, finally, that it is likely that most of these offenses will be committed in the governmental sector. The government is generally in the business of distributing subsidies, privileges, and burdens to individuals in the society as a matter of right. Moreover, the government officials typically act in situations in which explicit rules are supposed to define fully the nature of the transaction but where there is in fact enormous de facto discretion. In the sheer magnitude of the government enterprise and in the tension between the expectation that the transactions should proceed according to explicit rules and the actual experience of their subjective nature, there are vast opportunities for victimization by officials. Thus while there may be contracting and hiring abuses in both government and private sectors, probably the largest number of these offenses will occur within governmental institutions.

Embezzlement and Employee Fraud

The Nature of the Offense. A fourth component of the white-collar-crime problem can be called "embezzlement and employee fraud." This component introduces an interesting new relationship among offenders, victims, and institutions. So far in examining offenses committed by people with institutional positions, we have looked at their capacity to victimize individuals *outside* the institution—that is, consumers, clients, and suppliers. Starting with this component of the white-collar crime, we will be interested in a second possibility: that individuals in institutional positions can victimize their own institutions rather than its clients, consumers, or suppliers. Embezzlement is the paradigmatic offense: an individual within an institution exploits his control over the assets of an organization to take them for himself. It resembles pilfering except that the mechanism is deception rather than trespass.

There is a significant conceptual problem in trying to calibrate the seriousness of these offenses. It is clear, of course, that large amounts of money can be stolen by embezzlers or people who pay payrolls. But who is the victim in these offenses? The answer seems to be the organization itself. Of course there are individual victims in the form of clients, or owners and managers of the organizations. But the losses will be distributed among a large number of such individuals. Moreover, these individuals may never discover that they have been victimized. In effect, the organization serves to diffuse and disguise the losses. In my view, the fact that the losses are distributed over large numbers of individuals and well disguised *does* mitigate the seriousness of the offense. We care less about an offense that distributes $1,000 in losses among 1,000 relatively well-to-do organizational clients than a different offense that inflicts a $1,000 loss on a single person with limited means. In effect, since the victimization involves only money, is distributed among a large enough group to make the economic loss to each individual quite small, and neither humiliates nor frightens the victims, these offenses may not merit a great deal of social concern relative to others.

I suspect that our most fundamental interest in this area is the symbolic issue of equity rather than the substantive problem of victimization. It seems outrageously unfair that the opportunity to steal efficiently should be as unequally distributed as everything else in the society. It seems wrong that people in privileged positions with a stroke of a pen can steal thousands of dollars distributed over large numbers of unseeing, uncaring people while a person with a less advantaged position must rely on the much less efficient procedure of going from individual to individual and either sneaking their property away or attacking them. Since it seems so unfair, we should show some zeal in attacking these offenses even though the substantive stakes associated with victimization are not all that significant.

Control Possibilities. Moreover, in thinking about effective methods of control, it becomes apparent that the criminal-justice system may not have to play a very large role. On one hand, we realize that it is virtually impossible for the criminal-justice system to detect these offenses. The vast area in which these offenses could occur and the difficulty of seeing the offenses in the enormous volume of transactions executed (and recorded) by an institution, make it hopeless for the criminal-justice system to patrol for these offenses. On the other hand, we realize that the institutions themselves have both a strong interest and a capability in preventing and detecting the offenses themselves. After all, the problem of employee theft in an old one, and accounting has become a very sophisticated mechanism in response. It is likely then that our ability to control these kinds of offenses will depend almost entirely on the strength of the internal-control mechanisms of the institutions themselves: Organizations with strong internal controls will rarely be victimized; those with weaker controls will suffer often.

This simple observation about the kinds of institutions that will be victimized may imply that *government* agencies will be unusually vulnerable. They handle large amounts of money and for the most part have relatively weak accounting and auditing procedures. Thus the development of stronger accounting and auditing procedures within governmental institutions should probably be a high-priority matter in dealing with this component of white-collar crime. (It is for this reason that current legislation creating new offices of inspector generals in various federal departments should be welcomed.)

Note that our dependence on the interests and capabilities of the organizations themselves to deter and identify these kinds of white-collar crimes is not necessarily bad in terms of our *substantive* objectives. The organizations may do an excellent job of controlling the offenses. It may be bad, however, with respect to our *symbolic* objectives. The reason is simply that the victimized organizations may prefer to deal with the offenses privately and discreetly. This would be true if the organization wished to avoid punishing a valued colleague too harshly or if it would prove embarrassing to the organization to reveal its vulnerability. Regardless of the motives, however, if victimized organizations deal with offenders through firing, demotions, or other economic and personal humiliations, the criminal-justice system is cheated of its opportunity to show its willingness to punish such offenders in ways that are similar to our punishment of street criminals.

Thus to reassure ourselves that our criminal-justice system is prepared to punish people who use powerful organizational positions to steal as well as people who use force or stealth, we must find some way of dealing with the kinds of white-collar offenses that involve the victimization of organizations (and indirectly, their clients, owners, contributors, employees, or subjects) by people who occupy significant positions within them. Our ability to cope *substantively* with offenses of this type is particularly dependent on the internal-control systems of the governmental and economic organizations of our society. Our ability to cope *symbolically* with these offenses will depend on the willingness of the organizations to turn some of the cases they discover over to the criminal-justice system for prosecution. It is very difficult for the criminal-justice system itself to take any initiative in this area.

"Client Frauds"

A fifth component of white-collar crime involves stealing by economic *clients* or organizations that (in some sense at least) advance credit to their clients. Included in this component are credit-card fraud, insurance fraud, fraud by individual clients of welfare and medicare programs, and tax evasion. These offenses belong together because they involve an organization that distributes liabilities over *its* resources to a large number of individual clients or debtors who may take advantage of their control over that liability to steal resources from the institution.

This component of the problem turns out to be a close analogue to the problem of embezzlement and employee theft. There is the same difficulty in identifying who has been victimized and the same sense that the victimization is not so serious. Moreover, one is tempted to conclude that the major portion of the responsibility for controlling these offenses ought to lie with the institutions themselves. Their business involves distributing their resources and credit to individual clients. If they are vulnerable to client fraud, they are not performing their fundamental tasks effectively. Hence they should not be able to rely on the criminal-justice system to do a major part of their job. Finally, it is likely that if we should use criminal-justice resources anywhere in this system, we should begin with protecting public and governmental institutions. In fact, it is likely that tax evasion is overwhelmingly the most important offense in this area of white-collar crime. So the analysis of employee fraud is almost exactly duplicated for the problem of client fraud.

"Influence Peddling and Bribery"

A sixth component of the white-collar-crime problem involves individuals' with institutional positions selling their power, influence, and information to outsiders who have an interest in influencing or predicting the activities of the institution. Paradigmatic offenses here include kickbacks from contractors (who would not win the contract by merit) and SEC officials who sell information about planned SEC actions. In offenses like these, it is the organization that is victimized because its internal processes (which are presumably designed to allow it to perform its functions effectively and efficiently) are sabotaged by its own employees for their own interests. Unlike the case of embezzlement, it is not so much the institution's *assets* that are stolen, as its capacity to operate fairly and efficiently.

The victims of offenses of this type are the people who were competing with the interests that managed to achieve "undue influence" through their use of "bribery." It is less aggressive contractors who failed to buy off the contracting official or less aggressive lobbyists who were reluctant to pay crooked congressmen. Chances are, these people may suspect they have been victimized, but they may be unable to produce any evidence. In fact, these offenses will probably be extremely difficult to root out because no one who participates in the offense will have any incentive to come forward. Both the briber and the bribe receiver like things the way they are. Consequently, our response will depend crucially on the institutions themselves, perhaps aided on occasion by competitors who suspect they have been victimized and an aggressive investigative press that thrives on stories of scandal. Were all these to act together, the criminal-justice system might have an opportunity to intervene.

Note that these offenses are likely to be most serious where they occur within governmental institutions. The reasons are both substantive and symbolic. Where the government makes policy decisions governing the use of its enormous resources and authority to accomplish public purposes, a great many people are affected. Losses and gains in individual well-being are registered throughout the society. For those who lose (and sometimes even those who win), it is crucial to their sense of well-being that they believe that these decisions were made fairly and equitably. When these processes are manipulated by corrupt practices such as influence peddling and bribery, it is likely that our citizens will suffer unnecessary substantive losses and that their faith in the fairness at our governmental system will be eroded.

*Willful Noncompliance with Rules Regulating the
Conduct of Economic, Political, and Governmental
Institutions*

The Nature of the Offense. The last component of white-collar crime is probably the most challenging. It involves situations where powerful institutions (or individuals acting on behalf of powerful institutions) willfully violate laws that restrain the institutions from doing social harm or that require them to do social good.

This area too is potentially vast. We now have a great many laws designed to guarantee the ultimate benignity of our economic, political, and governmental processes. For example, in the *economic* arena we have laws to promote competition, to require various products to meet rigorous standards of safety and efficacy, to restrain false advertising, and to obligate firms to use safe and clean production processes. In the political arena we have laws regulating the registration of voters, the accessibility of candidates to the media, the use of public employees in politics, and the financing of political campaigns. And in the *governmental* arena, we have laws designed to assure widespread participation in major public-policy decisions (for example, the Administrative Procedures Act and the Freedom of Information Act), to protect the privacy of individual citizens, and to prevent obvious conflicts of interest among governmental officials. Moreover, cutting across both governmental and economic institutions, we have laws designed to achieve broad social purposes such as those that establish mandatory minimum wages, insist on nondiscrimination in hiring and selling, and protect long-term pension rights of employees. While most of the enforcement activity under these laws occurs through regulatory agencies relying on civil procedures, many of the laws do impose criminal sanctions for some kinds of violations.

The number and variety of these laws make it difficult to say much in general about the magnitude and character of the victimization that occurs as a result of criminal violations of these statutes. Clearly, losses in this area can be enormous. Price fixing is alleged to cost the consumer billions of dollars each year. Negligence in the production of lawnmowers, drugs, canned foods, cars, and airplanes, or willful disregard of environmental laws can result in substantial physical harm. And civil rights violations have struck at the very heart of our freedom, personal dignity and sense of security.

Moreover, a special kind of terror is associated with being abused and victimized by a large institution. One may find himself surrounded by others who are also victimized and peer into a future where no one comes to the rescue and the institution may become so pervasive and persistent that one ceases to experience his losses as victimization and accepts them as an unfortunate but inevitable feature of the world. Of course, things do not often get this bad. But when they do, the experience of the victimization is very severe. (Ironically, the experience may be so severe that it will be difficult to find anyone who will complain.)

Larded among spectacular offenses committed by negligent, clumsy, or willfully malevolent institutions, however, are a great many offenses that are less spectacular. The losses occur on a smaller scale with fewer portenses for the future. For these offenses, our stakes are likely to be more symbolic than substantive. Our symbolic stakes in these relatively insignificant cases arise from three different sources. One source is simply our desire to show our determination to regulate institutions in the areas where we have passed criminal statutes. We want to show that we were serious in imposing the new obligations and that the society has the will and the capacity to control its various institutions. A second source is indignation about the bad moral character of leaders of institutions who authorize cheating on their clearly mandated social responsibilities. We hate to believe that we are led and organized by people who will not accept the social responsibilities implicit in the laws. A third source is a desire to reassure ourselves about the fairness of the criminal-justice system. We want violations of criminal statutes to be punished regardless of the status of the offender or the seriousness of the offense. For all these reasons, we may sometimes want criminal prosecutions for willful violations of regulatory programs even for relatively trivial offenses.

Control Possibilities. In organizing a response to willful (or negligent) violations of socially mandated responsibilities, the criminal-justice system is again likely to play only a minor role. Much of the effective control over these offenses will depend on voluntary compliance by the affected institutions, and regulatory efforts managed largely through noncriminal investigations and sanctions. These mechanisms will act on a much larger scale than the criminal-justice system could ever hope to. In fact, the criminal-justice system will find it difficult both to identify offenses and offenders in this area.

The offenses may be relatively invisible for the same reason that embezzlement and client fraud are hard to see. The organization distributes the losses over a group of individuals large enough that no individual has a strong incentive to complain. Even if individuals notice they have been victimized, they may weigh the strength of their individual complaint against the power of the institution and quickly decide that the complaint is not worth the trouble. In fact, this situation is worse than the case of embezzlement and client fraud because in those cases we would at least rely on the institution itself to help us do the policing. In this case, however, the organization is no longer the victim, but the offender! So it has no incentive to help us locate the offenses. The only actor in a position to help the criminal-justice system identify offenses are the regulatory agencies who will occasionally encounter criminal misconduct in the course of their investigations. Given historically difficult relationships between regulatory agencies and criminal-justice agencies *and* given the general reluctance of regulatory agencies to threaten carefully nurtured relations with the regulated industries by referring cases for criminal prosecution, however, the regulatory agencies are not likely to turn many cases over to the criminal-justice system.

The offenders are likely to be relatively invisible because it will ordinarily be unclear who within the organization is responsible for the violations. Who, after all, are the guilty individuals if an organization's policy is to violate the laws? How will we know when officers of the organization were merely following explicit or implicit orders from supervisors and when they are assuming responsibility for their actions themselves? These problems are central to cases such as the price-fixing case in the electrical industry, the "black-bag" cases now being prosecuted within the FBI, and even the war trials at Nuremburg. The fact of the matter is that we do not now have a sensible, widely understood, easily applied rule that distributes legal and moral responsibility for organizationally sanctioned or motivated action among individuals within the organization. Without such rules, it is as hard to locate offenders as offenses in this area of white-collar crime.

Thus this last component of white-collar crime presents some of the knottiest problems in the entire area. I suspect that our substantive and symbolic stakes are greater in this area than in any other component of white-collar crime. The material and psychological losses to victims are significant when viewed in both individual and social terms. Moreover, these losses occur against the backdrop of a widespread social concern about our ability to control the behavior of large institutions. We have tried to indicate our determination in this area by establishing criminal sanctions and lashing out at leaders of institutions who violated those statutes. But our actions in this area may appear to be capricious partly because it is difficult to detect the offenses, partly because trivial, technical offenses are included among the more serious and partly because it is difficult to assign guilt to individuals within large organizations. I suspect progress in designing policy to deal with this component of white-collar crime depends on: (1) deciding which few among the rapidly proliferating regulatory programs involve the most important social concerns; (2) determining how the regulatory processes should be coordinated with the criminal procedures to maximize our ability to guide institutions in the regulated area; and (3) developing a reasonable principle for assigning guilt to individuals in cases that go to criminal prosecution. Despite the importance of this component of white-collar crime, no one appears to be working on this agenda.

Conclusion

This broad survey of the social concerns and diverse problems associated with the concept of white-collar crime is far from sufficient to support the detailed design of a national strategy. Still a few strategic principles emerge.

The first principle is that we have both substantive and symbolic objectives in this area. The substantive objectives involve reducing the victimization associated with white-collar offenses. We want to reduce the number of people who are injured or frightened or who lose money as a result of deception or exploitation of a superior bargaining position. The symbolic objectives involve reassuring ourselves about the fairness and consistency of the criminal-justice system. We want to see evidence that the criminal-justice system will treat deception and abuses of institutional position as harshly as stealth and physical attack and that it is willing to punish privileged and powerful offenders as well as those who are relatively powerless. To some extent, of course, the concept of deterrence relates the two different kinds of objectives: Cases prosecuted largely for symbolic purposes may produce real substantive results. Analytically, however, the two objectives are distinct. A relatively greater commitment to one objective or the other would shift our white-collar crime strategy significantly. A commitment to substantive objectives would focus our attention on individual abuses of institutional positions, and major offenses involving willful institutional noncompliance with socially established obligations. A commitment to symbolic objectives might leave more room for efforts directed against embezzlement and employee fraud. Thus, the two different kinds of concerns can powerfully influence the focus of a national strategy toward white-collar crime.

The distinction between the two kinds of objectives is important not only because it raises the crucial issue of which offenses are relatively more important to attack, but also because it raises a second crucial issue in the design of a national strategy: namely, a calculation about the appropriate division of labor between the criminal-justice system and all other mechanisms of social control in coping with white-collar offenses. To the extent that we want to achieve substantive results, we may want to keep *most* of the responsibility for the control of white-collar offenses within the larger and less-formal mechanisms of control that exist outside the criminal-justice system. To the extent that we want to achieve symbolic goals, we will be tempted to bring some portion of these cases into the criminal-justice system. Calculating the number of cases to be handled in the criminal-justice system that is at once large enough to achieve symbolic and deterrence objectives, and small enough to guarantee that other agencies and systems continue to feel responsible for *substantive* control of the offenses must be a key part of our policy toward white-collar crime. My feeling is that the right number of cases will be a very small number within the criminal-justice system. Given the vastness of the area, and the comparative advantage of other institutions in detecting and controlling the offenses, the interest of the criminal-justice system may turn out to be almost entirely symbolic. Thus, the second strategic principle is that the criminal-justice system should not become so active against white-collar crime that other agencies now assisting in the substantive control of white-collar offenses slacken their current efforts: our first line of defense against embezzlement must be continued vigilance by banks.

A third strategic principle that emerges from the analysis is that exploitation of a superior bargaining position is as important a mechanism of white-collar crime as deception. The experience of victimization is likely to be extremely unpleasant. Moreover, the mechanism seems to be at the heart of many of the resentments and fears stimulated by people who exploit an institutional position to injure us. Finally, I would expect this problem to grow as the society becomes increasingly organized and regulated. For all these reasons, I would urge that we pay attention to exploitation as well as deception.

A fourth principle developed in the discussion is that governmental and political institutions are scarcely immune from white-collar offenses. They are clearly vulnerable to embezzlement, employee fraud, and client fraud just as private economic institutions are. And in the crucial area of individual abuses of authority, bribery, and willful institutional noncompliance, the problems within governmental institutions are likely to be at least as significant as within private. At a substantive level then, governmental and political institutions house a major part of the problem.

At a symbolic level, I think offenses within governmental and political institutions are even more important. The government has always had a slightly different moral status than private enterprise. We give it this status because we want the officials and institutions to feel more than ordinarily responsible. After all, they are dealing in two very abusable commodities—power and other peoples' money. Hence we insist on higher standards and ought to be more concerned when fraud, theft, and extortion appear in governmental processes than when they appear in private economic activity. Moreover, it is more than a little hypocritical for government agencies to attack private economic institutions for offenses that they ignore when they occur in governmental agencies. In short, far from being outside the scope of white-collar crime, offenses committed with governmental and political institutions are at the very core of the problem.

A fifth "principle" (more in the nature of a worry than an established principle) is that our current planning efforts and organizational development efforts may be targeted on the wrong piece of the problem. Our current efforts in this area are designed primarily to deal with fraud and embezzlement in both private and governmental sectors. I am worried that we will work hard in this area and ignore what appear to me to be the crucial problems of abuses of institutional position, bribery, and institutional noncompliance with social obligations. If I am right about the relative importance of these offenses in the general area of white-collar crime, it seems crucial to me that we begin thinking about the problem of criminal enforcement of existing social regulations as well as fraud and embezzlement. It is in this area that I think the most important programmatic challenges to a white-collar-crime-containment strategy may lie.

4 The Institutional Challenge of White-Collar Crime

Marilyn E. Walsh

The stated purpose of this volume is to explore the breadth of the social challenge presented by the problem of white-collar crime. This purpose was adopted in recognition of the fact that the criminal-justice system, standing alone, is neither uniquely challenged by white-collar crime nor uniquely responsible for its containment. Instead, white-collar crime tears at the fabric of a broad range of social, political, and economic institutions; and all these must share in some measure the responsibility and the burden of coping with it.

Mark Moore, the author of chapter 3, began by stating an intriguing premise. Increasingly, suggested Moore, the automatic response to victimization within and through basic institutions in society (his definition of white-collar crime) has been a monolithic one: that of extending criminal liability to such victimizing conduct. And all too often, continued Moore, the criminal-justice system has either fostered or acquiesced in this approach.

Such criminal-justice-system support or acceptance of a containment model dominated by criminal sanctions has been in apparent disregard, noted Moore, of two important implications of adopting this approach. First, use of the criminal sanction to control and preserve the benevolence of basic institutions shifts entirely the resources burden for such efforts to the public sector. Second, extensions of criminal liability into more and more areas of organizational and institutional misconduct only sharpens the symbolic significance of having such white-collar-crime cases vigorously investigated and prosecuted. This heightened symbolic need for action thereby increases the resource requirements for white-collar-crime control efforts to a point where the burden on the public sector is neither economically feasible nor politically likely. The criminal-justice system then, by an unquestioning encouragement and/or acceptance of a *criminal*-containment policy for white-collar crime, has set itself up to fail. It has accepted a challenge and raised expectations that it can in no way meet.

Of particular interest in all of this, continued Moore, is the fact that the criminal-justice system has doomed itself to failure by neglecting to take proper cognizance of the one critical aspect of the white-collar-crime challenge it best understands, that is, the fact that a widely varied range of conduct is subsumed under the white-collar-crime rubric. Had the criminal-justice system properly recognized this aspect of the white-collar-crime challenge, noted Moore, then it would have realized as well that the different types of white-collar crime of concern to society call for a more varied and in some cases less dominant set of roles for enforcement authorities than the monolithic one envisioned by a criminal-containment model.

Moore presented his own typology of white-collar crime, illustrative of the varied roles in which the criminal-justice system might be cast with respect to white-collar-crime containment. At the one end of the white-collar-crime spectrum, noted Moore, are the acts of individual fraud operators victimizing other individuals. Here the criminal-justice system is cast in its traditional enforcement role of responding to victim complaints. Note, however, that this role envisions a partnership between the criminal-justice system and victims in controlling white-collar crime—it does not expect the criminal-justice system to have the full burden of responsibility for containing such acts.

A second type of white-collar crime, conceptually midway in the spectrum, consists of individual actors either within or outside of institutional structures victimizing those structures. Here, noted Moore, the role of the criminal-justice system is at best a minor one. For while there may be some symbolic stakes involved in having the criminal-justice system handle a few such cases, it is also clear that the substantive job of controlling this type of white-collar-crime conduct must be left to those organizations and institutions who are victimized. For this part of the white-collar-crime problem then, no dominant or exclusive role for the criminal-justice system should be expected.

Finally, according to Moore's typology, there are white-collar crimes in which organizations and institutions, through conscious policies, are the offenders. Here, from Moore's perspective, is found the greatest challenge to the criminal-justice system. Here both the symbolic and the substantive stakes in criminal-justice-system effectiveness are the highest. And here society has no real alternative but the criminal-justice system to take responsibility for controlling such conduct. If there is any aspect of the white-collar-crime problem where the criminal-justice system should be expected to play an exclusive, dominant role, it is where organizational mal- and misfeasance are concerned.

Moore's discussion provokes three issues of debate. First, one can take issue with his contention that the criminal-justice system is on a collision course with failure in its white-collar-crime control efforts and, in particular, that the system has put itself on such a course. With respect to the first of these contentions, such statements can be considered gratuitous and productive only of defeatism—something not needed, given the large challenge presented by white-collar crime. These troubled by the concept of unavoidable failure may also feel that such a perspective results from a misinterpretation of the apparent dominance of the criminal-justice system. The criminal-justice system is "out front" in white-collar-crime-control efforts after all, in much the same way that it can be viewed as dominating efforts to contain other crime problems. But this dominance translates to a leadership role that the criminal-justice system is expected to play and should play—not an attempt to preempt others or to exert exclusive intervention. Society looks to the criminal-justice system to provide leadership and to set the tone from crime-control programs. By assuming that role, the system does not claim exclusive responsibility nor should it be expected to behave that way.

On the other hand, given the importance of the leadership function, one might question whether the criminal-justice system could walk away from certain areas of white-collar crime, leaving the responsibility to others, as Moore's typology suggested. Thus while Moore's model, if accepted, would carve out a smaller area of responsibility for white-collar-crime control within which the criminal-justice system might expect to be more effective, the system probably could not really take such a position, given not only social and political expectations but also the realities of self-policing in public and private institutions without criminal-justice-system involvement. Is it at all socially responsible for the criminal-justice system to walk away from areas of widespread abuse knowing that the slack is not likely to be picked up by others?

Also questionable is the second part of Moore's "failure" contention, that is, that the criminal-justice system had through direct action or acquiescense, put itself on a destructive course. This notion is widely disputed. To begin with, the criminal-justice system is and has been for some time open to noncriminal sanctioning alternatives. Similarly, many in the criminal-justice system for some time have been leery of and argued against expansions of criminal liability into new areas of white-collar-crime conduct. Still the power and the deterrent potential of the criminal sanction in white-collar-crime areas must be recognized and reckoned with as an effective containment mechanism. Congress knows this as do many state legislatures. Much expansion of criminal liability into new areas then as has been in recognition of the fact that this mechanism is probably the most efficient tool available for containing abusive conduct.

The problem, however, is not the expansion of criminal liability but rather the failure on the part of legislative authorities to provide the criminal-justice system with adequate resources to successfully police new areas of responsibility. Thus enabling legislation in areas of social regulation such as environmental pollution may establish criminal penalties but rarely provide mechanisms such as special reporting or certification requirements that would surface violations and make policing more effective and efficient. Any failures here cannot be laid at the doorstep of the criminal-justice system that recognizes these needs but rather must be laid at the feet of legislative authorities. The criminal-justice system, however, if given adequate resources and procedural requirements, could absorb new areas of responsibility.

A second major area of concern emerges from Moore's suggestion that responsibility for controlling abuses of institutions by individuals could be shifted entirely to those institutions, with the criminal-justice system's acting only when called on by institutional victims themselves—as in the case of individual victimization. In general, there are serious drawbacks to such a proposition. Of particular concern is the traditional reluctance—indeed resistance—of private-sector institutions to report instances of abuse. Often there is little incentive to do so, but even where economic incentives to ferret out and report abuses do exist, there are other motivations—fear of embarrassment, loss of business, or a desire to cover up problems—that generally impede institutional victims from coming forward. Reliance on self-reporting by those within institutions then would be tantamount to ignoring this whole portion of the white-collar-crime problem. The viability of this posture is questionable with respect to individual victims, many of whom fail to report abuses because they remain unaware of their victimization or are impeded out of embarrassment or guilt. But if individual victims suffering direct personal losses cannot be relied on to seek official assistance, how confident can one be that those in organizational positions will report abuses when it is the organization that is victimized?

One could of course take the position that victims unwilling to come forward cannot and should not expect redress. This position has not been well accepted with respect to individual victims and should not be adopted regarding institutional victims. With respect to individual victims, the view is not well accepted because such victims are often not in the best position to determine what has happened to them or how they should proceed. With respect to institutional victims, however, the situation is more complex and the implications of relying only on self-policing and reporting are more serious. This is because those within institutions (that is, managers, administrators) who must decide whether or not to report abuses may not have a personal stake in doing so; while those who do have a personal stake in discovering and reporting abuses (that is, stockholders, customers, competitors, and so on) are unlikely to be in a position or have the information necessary to do so. Thus since the interest of those within institutions who have the ability to surface and report abuses are not identical—or even similar in some cases—to those who may suffer the consequences of such abuses, a posture of responding only to reported institutional victimization cannot be considered statisfactory.

A third issue raised by Moore concerns the other obvious alternative that would achieve control of abuse and still keep responsibility for that control within institutions. This alternative consists of creating legal or extralegal obligations on the part of individuals within institutions to surface and report abuses. The spectre of a society of informants that this alternative raises is quite disturbing. There is a distinction between imposing reporting requirements on institutions, thereby creating organizational obligations, and imposing them on individuals within institutions, creating individual obligations. In the latter instance one can well imagine the situation in which concerns over personal liability might prevent individuals from performing normal organizational functions.

Given the preceding questions about Moore's premises, it is safe to conclude that the criminal-justice system cannot abandon responsibility for oversight and control of institutional victimization. This conclusion does not, however, adequately address the issue giving rise to Moore's premise, that is, the freely acknowledged fact that the criminal-justice system must (in order to do its job) rely for enforcement assistance on institutional structures that are presently somewhat unmotivated to provide needed assistance. While disputing Moore's solution then, it is true that the issue of institutional support of and assistance to official white-collar-crime-containment efforts is indeed a serious one. The formulation of a solution alternative to that presented by Moore remains, however, beyond our grasp. Instead, the following suggestions may be considered. First, expanded and more imaginative use of compliance procedures (in particular, such measures as SEC registration filings) could provide enforcement authorities, whether criminal, civil, or administrative, with monitoring information that could serve as a basis for control efforts. Second, extensions of the affirmative duties of officials in institutions and organizations should be explored. (It should be reemphasized here that such duties should be institutional rather than individual in character.) Finally, private, extralegal sanctioning accomplished by institutions and professional groups might be better publicized by enforcement authorities as part of a broader social program to control white-collar crime. A corollary to this latter point would urge enforcement authorities to work more closely with professional groups to help structure and support their sanctioning activities and with institutions and organizations to improve and strengthen internal-control procedures.

A final area of concern raised by Moore's discussion concerns the segment of the white-collar-crime problem involving conscious acts of misfeasance or malfeasance by whole institutions or organizations, which Moore suggests should be a major responsibility of the criminal-justice system. There is grave concern here that such a policy would place enforcement authorities in the position of making decisions outside their area of knowledge and expertise. Currently, the justice system is called on to make enforcement decisions in such areas as pollution control, for example, that have widespread economic implications. Those put in that position express great discomfort and concern at being asked to be economic policy makers. "Should I as an enforcement official be empowered to decide that 8,000 will be put out of work?" is an example of the type of question raised. Similar examples exist in which enforcement actions are closely connected to foreign policy or other considerations beyond the scope of expertise of criminal-justice-system personnel. The notion that enforcement authorities could act in isolation without taking account of such considerations can be rejected; and the idea that the criminal-justice system should be expected to make decisions having such widespread ramifications is questionable.

Considering then who should make such decisions, the answer may be that legislative authorities should bear this burden. For example, legislative authorities might be asked to enunciate policy guidelines within which enforcement personnel could then appropriately exert their authority. But to lodge major decisions of an economic or foreign-policy nature in the criminal-justice system seems both unwise and inappropriate.

Of major concern are abuses in the public sector that can properly be called white-collar crime; however, the capacity of public-sector institutions to surface and adequately control such abuse is perhaps not as important as other problems. Pointed toward as contributing to a greater confidence in public institutions are: (1) positions in government agencies such as that of an inspector general—a functionary that has no parallel privately; (2) the fishbowl environment in which public officials operate (which is much less common for officials in private organizations); and (3) the higher standards of conduct expected of public officials and insured by either specific legislation or the election process.

In general, the public sector can be viewed as possessing check-and-balance mechanisms more suited to containing white-collar crime than those to be found in the private sector. The larger problem with respect to organizational wrongdoing is not the public sector per se but rather the interaction between the complex array of public institutions (civil, administrative, and criminal) and the private sector. It is in this interaction that the varied—and often conflicting—goals of administrative versus criminal-enforcement agencies, for example, may give the appearance that uneven and unequal justice is being rendered.

The symbolic stakes attached to better coordination of the policy guidelines of public agencies therefore has been crucial. Too often, however, the competing or conflicting objectives of various public agencies are not easily conformed to each other. Nor are moves to coordinate policy always readily or voluntarily accepted. Rather, public agencies are often quite sensitive to having their internal policies dictated by others, even in the name of accommodating a broader set of policy guidelines. A key hurdle to be overcome in developing a national strategy for white-collar-crime containment then is the effective balancing of the need for coherent policy coordination among public agencies against the need to maintain the integrity and independence of the varied agencies with their separable charters, objectives, and jurisdictions that may be involved.

There are numerous examples of instances in which the decisions of administrative regulatory bodies result in enforcement outcomes that fall short of criminal sanctions, though such sanctions could have been invoked. In such cases the actual outcomes may give the appearance that certain offenders have received unequal, favored treatment at the hands of government when, in fact, the outcomes represent thoroughly proper exercises of regulatory discretion. Some criminal-justice agencies feel, however, that clearer policy guidelines cutting across agencies would result in more consistent and coherent enforcement responses to the white-collar-crime problem and would minimize those situations where significantly different outcomes occur in similar cases.

**Part III
The Role of the
Criminal-Justice System in
Containing White-Collar Crime**

5 White-Collar Crime and the Criminal-Justice System: Problems and Challenges

Daniel L. Skoler

Our experts in white-collar crime have a habit—a laudable one—of stressing that white-collar crime is indeed crime, pure and unadulterated. This is of course true; and thus, despite special linkages with, and options of, regulatory enforcement and a variety of civil-sanction measures and techniques, the major arena and front stage for addressing white-collar deviancy must be the nation's official apparatus for dealing with criminal behavior—our criminal-justice system (or "nonsystem" depending on one's intellectual inclinations). [The term "criminal-justice system," as used here, refers to the complete complex of criminal-administration components (police, prosecution, courts, corrections, criminal defense) at all government levels (federal, state, county, municipal) with special emphasis on enforcement and prosecution functions.]

In the United States the criminal-justice system is a huge, multifaceted, many-tiered, decentralized goliath, most of it—in dollar and manpower terms—focused and operating at state, county, and municipal levels. Precious little attention has been lavished on the roles, responsibilities, and priorities of these "line actors" with respect to white-collar crime, in no small part due to an overriding (and quite legitimate) preoccupation with street crime, organized crime, and violent acts. That is why contributions like the Justice Department's new white-collar-crime-investigation manual with its explicit guidance for the "bread-and-butter" components of law enforcement in their day-to-day operations are so critical and so needed (patrol, investigation, business and community relations, internal organization and specialization, and so on).[1]

The purpose of this chapter is to examine white-collar-crime containment in terms of systemwide approaches, issues, coordination, and impacts. The discussion will initially be descriptive and thereafter analytical and speculative, recognizing that only surfaces can be scratched with this important subject. The special influence of federal legislation and regulation and the special responsibilities vested in administrative departments and agencies which are primarily engaged in criminal-justice or law-enforcement endeavors in this field, create almost unique interface and coordination problems for criminal-justice systems.

The White-Collar-Crime Problem

White-collar crime pervades American society, imposes enormous social and economic costs, impacts on the disadvantaged and the many as deeply and destructively as on the affluent and the few, and yet, it seems fair to say, attracts a disproportionately small share of criminal-justice resources, manpower, attention, and coordination.

The literature is neither wanting nor less-than-persuasive on this proposition and the definitional parameters of this species of criminal activity, thoughtfully examined, almost make a self-evident case. Ignoring the old Sutherland "character-of-the-offender" definition (the high status and respectable actor) in favor of the justice department-endorsed, now widely accepted, and more fundamental "character-of-the-act" formulation, that is,

> an illegal act or series of illegal acts committed by non-physical means and by concealment or guile, to obtain money or property, to avoid the payment or loss of money or property, or to obtain business or personal advantage. . . ,

we can play out the common varieties of white-collar crime and then begin to examine their treatment at the hands of the system. As sorted out by Herbert Edelhertz, these crimes fall into four general categories:

1. *Ad-hoc violations:* committed for personal benefit on an episodic basis. (Examples would be tax fraud or welfare frauds.)
2. *Abuses of trust:* committed by a fiduciary or trusted agent or employee. (Examples would be embezzlement or the receipt of a bribe, kickback, or favor to confer a benefit.)
3. *Collateral business crimes:* committed by businesses to further their legitimate primary purposes. (Examples would be antitrust violations, bribery of customers' agents, use of false weights and measures, concealment of adverse environmental- and drug-test findings, and sale misrepresentations.)
4. *Con games:* committed for the sole purpose of cheating customers. (Examples would be charity frauds, land-sale frauds, and sale of worthless securities or business opportunities.)[2]

Perhaps symptomatic of the collateral status accorded white-collar crime in our criminal-justice system thinking is the fact that current national reporting and statistical systems on crime and criminal justice, despite considerable growth and refinement in the past decade, offer few breakdowns on incidence, arrests, prosecutions, and other dispositions of white-collar offenses. Our most thorough and comprehensive crime-reporting system, the *FBI Uniform Crime Reports,* collects no data on reported white-collar-crime offenses, focusing instead on the seven "index offenses" (homicide, aggravated assault, rape, robbery, burglary, auto theft, and larceny theft). The largest of these numerically, that is, larceny theft (5.9 million of 1977's 11 million reported index offenses) probably includes some white-collar crimes but by FBI definition "fraud, embezzlement, con games, forgery, and worthless checks" are specifically excluded so that the number is probably not great. Indeed, no statistics are collected on these white-collar crimes although the *Uniform Crime Reports* do include tabulations of arrests for nonindex crimes, including the categories of "forgery and counterfeiting," "fraud," and "embezzlement," and the quasi-categories of "buying, receiving, possessing stolen property," and "arson" (the latter, along with several other crimes, involving frequent concealment or fraud dimensions). Reported arrests for these offenses in 1977 slightly exceeded 450,000 or 4.4 percent of the 10.2 million arrests classified by types of offense in the 1977 reports. While federal investigation, prosecution, and conviction statistics seem somewhat better, they are often diffused among a variety of reports and agency tabulations.[3]

Reliable and aggregated conviction data are even harder to come by, and only the federal prison system and a few states seem to maintain breakdowns of sentenced prisoners by type of crime identifiable for white-collar definitional purposes. For example, in 1975 some 1,200 federal prisoners of the 20,700 classified by offenses in Bureau of Prison statistics (total universe of 22,500) as of 30 June 1975 were serving time for essentially white-collar offenses.[4] This amounted to less than 6 percent of the federal prisoner population, probably a much higher figure than most states because of the greater state- and local-government focus on street crime.

The Criminal-Justice System

Although well known to professionals and students of the American criminal-justice system, a few facts about that system's size, shape, and character may help fix perspectives.

Today public crime-control expenditures aggregate approximately $22 billion annually, second only to education, health, and public welfare in domestic outlays. These costs are divided among the major functions into about 55 percent for police services, 25 percent for corrections, and 20 percent for courts (the latter including prosecution and defense). Most of these, over 85 percent, are state and local outlays; and the largest cost component, more than 85 percent, is personnel. In all areas of activity except corrections and despite increasing federal and state roles, local-government outlays substantially exceed those at federal and state levels (for example, more than twice as much for police protection as federal and state expenditures combined, about twice as much for judicial operation, and one and a half times as much for prosecution).

More than 1.1 million governmental employees are involved in operation of our law-enforcement apparatus: about 650,000 in police service, 250,000 in corrections, 150,000 in courts, 60,000 in prosecution and governmental legal services, and 8,000 in public defense. They deal with approximately 20 million reported crimes annually—about 11 million within the FBI's seven major index-crime categories—some 8 million police arrests annually, 1.5 million offenders in institutions or under supervision (of this group some 500,000 are confined in the nation's 600 adult and juvenile institutions and more than 4,000 local jails and juvenile-detention centers; the remainder are under probation, parole, or other community programs), and 4.5 to 6 million criminals- and juvenile-court cases. The evidence suggests that total crime, reported and unreported, should be two or three times larger than the known-offense figures and that beyond public expenditure, crime costs the nation in personal injury, stolen or damaged property, and concomitant economic loss more than $50 billion annually. Organized-crime revenues and white-collar-crime loss alone have been estimated (at least per "high-range" estimates) at close to that annual figure.

Reported major crime in the United States rose some 140 percent during the decade of the sixties and topped 200 percent in the span from 1960 to 1975. This represents an increase from 1,880 to over 5,000 per 100,000 population. Of the 11 million index crimes reported in 1977, about 1 million or roughly 9 percent were violent crimes (murder, assault, rape, and robbery), and 10 million were crimes of property (burglary, auto theft, and larceny). Crime continues to have an urban emphasis (a metropolitan-area rate of more than 5,800 per 100,000 compared with a national average of 5,000 and a rural rate of about 2,000) and a big-city emphasis (26 cities account for almost 25 percent of all reported major crimes and over 35 percent of violent crimes, with 20 cities' producing nearly half the robberies in the United States in 1977).

Despite the high volume of total arrests, the actual rate of major offenses cleared by arrest of an offender whether or not ultimately convicted, has been consistently less than 25 percent (about 21 percent in 1977) with somewhat better experience on violent crimes (46-percent clearance rate). Thus not much more than 2 million of 1976's 11 million major reported crimes were cleared by arrest. Although national statistics on prosecution and conviction are somewhat spotty beyond this point, evidence suggests, as has been the case for many years, that not more than 2 out of 10 major offenders are brought to justice for serious crime in this nation and less than one out of 10 is ever convicted of a criminal offense. Nevertheless, since many crimes are the work of a single career criminal or serious offender, a persuasive case can be made for the proposition that sooner or later virtually every regular repeater will be apprehended, adjudicated, and "do some time."[5]

In terms of structure, the picture is awesome. Our nation has close to 20,000 separate and independent police forces, about 2,700 prosecutorial units, and some 15,600 criminal courts (200 appellate, 3,400 general-jurisdiction trial courts, and 12,000 trial courts of special jurisdiction). As might be supposed, most of this organizational multiplicity is accounted for by units serving rural or low-population areas and most manpower and workload is concentrated in larger units serving populous areas. For example, the majority of police departments have less than 10 personnel (about 90 percent), but 150 of the largest police forces account for more than half of all police officers in the nation. Federal and state criminal-justice agencies are much less prolific than their county and municipal counterparts. The president's Reorganization Project identified some 112 federal agencies engaged in "police, law enforcement and investigative activities," only 12 of which were deemed to have primary law-enforcement missions (concluding, nevertheless, that too much overlap and fragmentation still exists).[6] We know, moreover, that there are only 50 state attorneys general, almost 50 state police forces (Hawaii does not have one and several states have separate investigative bureaus) and 50 state supreme courts (with intermediate appellate courts expanding rapidly and court-unification legislation gathering thousands of local courts into hierarchically ordered, state-administered structures).

Of those convicted of criminal offenses, the majority are adjudicated not through trial but rather by guilty pleas (60 to 80 percent in most jurisdictions). This is done typically as the result of plea bargains under which the accused admits guilt to the offense charged or to a lesser offense on the basis of some understanding with prosecutorial authorities of leniency in treatment or the likely penalty to be imposed by sentencing courts. Of those sentenced, our experience indicates that at least 2 out of 3 offenders will be punished without a jail or prison sentence, even for felony offenses, with the typical disposition being fine or probation. While for those imprisoned, court sentences in the United States are deemed quite long in comparison with other Western nations, actual time served for felony offenders will generally fall well under two years.

This then is the broad setting in which white-collar-crime-containment strategies, resource-allocation choices, and enforcement priorities must operate and compete—perhaps more than a match for any order of national "special-focus," crime-control programming.

Federal-Level Structure, Activities, and Dilemmas

On the federal level, as might be expected, there is a great deal of activity directed against white-collar crime.[7] This effort, however, has been impeded and probably diluted by structural and resource problems. White-collar-crime-containment is structured as follows:

Detection

Detection of white-collar crime is primarily in the hands of administrative departments and agencies. Thus prima facie evidence of any crime must be reported by federal agencies to the Department of Justice or to the FBI for investigation. In some instances, however (for example, the SEC or the Postal Service), federal agencies have their own investigative branches that refer cases directly to the prosecutive arms of the Department of Justice in Washington or to U.S. attorneys in the field.

Most detection is reactive, that is, generated in response to complaints. Some is proactive, as in the case of those SEC activities that involve monitoring market activity or corporate filings for signs of violations. Other government personnel-conduct audits (defense contractors, research grantees, businessmen qualifying for federal subsidies or credits, taxpayers, and so on) that have a high potential for identifying white-collar misconduct. However, except in a few rare instances (usually found in IRS or SEC operations), agency enforcement officials are hesitant to consider cases for criminal prosecution. Agents or auditors alert to criminal issues lose their zeal in continued confrontation with discouragement and delay or in the protracted course and politics of administrative and civil-settlement negotiation.

Investigation

Investigation of white-collar violations is conducted administratively within federal agencies and departments, and by the FBI. While levels of capability vary, they are often quite high. Nevertheless, the arena of investigation is limited by lack of funds, the restricted scope of some investigative authorizations, heavy caseloads, red tape, and concerns about how investigators' work products will be received and used by prosecutors who have discretion to prosecute or to decline prosecution. While it is true that federal criminal-justice expenditures have increased in greater proportion than those of state and local government since the turn of the seventies (and even more markedly for police and law-enforcement functions), the continuing "explosion" in federal-regulation and consumer-protection measures has probably more than neutralized any resource advantages accuring to the federal white-collar-crime-containment initiative.

Notwithstanding, an encouraging new priority for white-collar-crime containment appears to have found tangible support within the federal investigative community. Under new leadership, the FBI recently established white-collar cases as one of three major investigative priorities (along with foreign counterintelligence and organized crime), including the assignment of about 20 percent of the bureau's field manpower (some 1,500 agents as of mid;1979) to this mission.[8] This has been accompanied by an increased emphasis on computer crimes, major financial frauds, and other sophisticated white-collar offenses and the willingness to deploy the intensive resources necessary to deal with such crimes even though the yield in total criminal-case volume must necessarily suffer in annual FBI statistical scorecards.

Prosecution

Criminal prosecution is invariably conducted by U.S. attorneys and Department of Justice attorneys from the Criminal, Tax, Antitrust, and Civil Rights Divisions. Where a case is not strong enough or where discretion has been exercised against criminal prosecution for a valid or less justified reason, the same kind of case may often be prosecuted civilly or administratively by other federal departments and agencies.

Federal detection, investigation, and prosecution operate under substantial constraints that derive from problems of legal jurisdiction, lack of resources, and enforcement policies. For example, consumer protection is relatively uncoordinated at the federal level, with responsibilities placed in a host of agencies and departments. Many of these offices have simultaneous responsibility for policing, stimulating, and assuring the economic health and public confidence in the enterprises being monitored and, in so doing, often become vulnerable to the conflicts posed by such dual responsibility.

Antitrust enforcement is divided between the Department of Justice and the FTC, with each alternately assuming the lead. Sheer chance may determine whether a merchandising-fraud operator will be dealt with by the FTC (where a cease-and-desist order is likely to issue only after a period of several years) or will be criminally indicted and exposed to heavy fines or a possible prison sentence as a result of prosecution by the Department of Justice. While the FTC has shown great ingenuity in using the tools at its disposal, disparities of this kind often flow from the uncoordinated response to the white-collar-crime problem and generate justified concern.

Enforcement policies are of key importance. Not enough, for example, is done by the federal government in contract-renegotiation procedures to recapture excessive profits or to utilize renegotiation-audit procedures to unearth indications of procurement fraud. Audit and compliance activities within government programs unfortunately often require that numerous review and administrative hurdles be overcome before a case is referred for criminal prosecution or civil recovery. Broad "inward looks" and policy formulations on criminal prosecution such as that recently announced for the Justice Department's environmental-protection enforcement program can offer guidance and have salutory impacts on internal staff, officials of concerned regulatory agencies, and potential violators.[9]

How resources are made available will often determine whether the federal government means what is says about fighting white-collar crime. Audit operations of IRS and the Enforcement Division of the SEC, as well as the Antitrust Division of Justice are customarily strapped for funds, a situation that must convey undesired messages not only to taxpayers, the securities industry, and potential antitrust violators but also to the attorneys and accountants who represent and advise them.

It is not unusual to hear the judiciary, federal, or otherwise, criticized for applying different punishment yardsticks to white-collar offenders as compared to those who commit common crimes. The criticism is valid, but the responsibility must be shared. Courts do no more than reflect the existing overall climate of tolerance toward white-collar crime, as evidenced by legislative, executive, and private policies in this area.

The issue of private enforcement is rarely addressed in considering white-collar crime and yet this area offers a powerful resource for federal white-collar-crime containment. Large corporations and smaller businesses spend hundreds of millions of dollars each year on internal audits that could do more (as our courts have recognized) to deter and unearth white-collar crimes. The U.S. Chamber of Commerce, the insurance industry, and other sectors of the business community have mounted investigative and educational programs directed against white-collar crime. The containment value of all this is often limited by the reluctance of business to refer cases for criminal prosecution except in instances where no insider is culpably or negligently involved. This kind of consideration can never be completely countered by enforcement policy, but clear signals as to severe treatment of foot dragging where knowledge is clear can make a contribution.

Since the federal government is always sounding the trumpet of coordination and planning in its state-local assistance programs, some "religion" in its own white-collar-crime-containment planning and legislation would seem in order. Given the problems of lack of resources and "externalities" (benefits and costs beyond the interests and citizens meant to be affected), our lawmakers would do well to heed Deputy Attorney General Benjamin Civiletti's recent advice on new planning initiatives and internal policing of regulators as well as regulatees:

> We are concerned in the Executive Branch that the Congress can do more to prevent fraud. When a social welfare program is designed, too little emphasis is placed on beginning the flow of federal dollars. The Department of Justice is developing a concept in which Congress will consider the Law Enforcement Impact before adopting new social programs. Additionally, there is now pending in Congress legislation to establish Inspectors General in 11 different agencies. This will give a new thrust and vitality to actively seeking out fraud and corruption as well as abuse and waste (Grand Rapids Economic Club, May 1978).

[In October 1978 Congress enacted and the president approved Public Law 95–542 establishing inspector general offices, with broad powers and reporting directly to the agency heads and the Congress, as internal-audit and inspection units within five executive departments (Agriculture, Interior, Labor, Commerce, Transportation, and Housing and Urban Development) and six federal "administrations" (GSA, EPA, NASA, SBA, CSA, and VA). Following an earlier legislative initiative establishing the DHEW Inspector General (PL 94–506, 94th Congress), this brought under inspector general cognizance executive-branch programs involving expenditures of well over $100 billion annually and more than 600,000 federal employees. As of mid-1979, another legislative proposal to establish an umbrella inspection unit within the Department of Justice, that is, Office of Professional Responsibility, was also pending (HR 4121, 96th Congress, 1st Session).]

One final aspect of the federal effort offers a natural transition to the state and local enforcement arena. That involves the federal back-up role to the criminal-justice heartland—technical assistance, training, and grants-in-aid to enhance capabilities and stimulate priorities and attention for white-collar offenses. The primary impetus for this kind of federal endeavor has been the Omnibus Crime Control and Safe Streets Act of 1968, as amended, now operating a variety of subsidy, demonstration, research, technical assistance, and educational programs ($260 million level in 1970, $860 million in 1975, and $620 million today) and probably soon to be replaced by a reorganized grant-in-aid structure). Administered by the Justice Department's LEAA, for which crime on the streets has always been the major priority, limited funds and projects for white-collar-crime containment did begin to flow in 1973 after the consciousness-raising ordeal of Watergate.[10] However, such initiatives and funds have been altogether too modest and could be readily doubled or tripled without even rippling the waters of LEAA's street-crime priorities. Any such increased effort, if properly structured, could offer enormous return in multiplying state and local effectiveness in white-collar-crime containment. This, of course, would require sensitivity to the potentials, limitations, and realities of the state-local contribution.

State and Local Structure, Activities, and Dilemmas

As has been observed, the state and local criminal-justice apparatus is much larger than that of the federal government. White-collar-crime-containment activities, however, are probably at a much lower level and that is understandable. Besides the obvious competition with street crime and organized crime, it is in the nature of a large segment of white-collar crime to victimize people in many jurisdictions, to be viewed less as a purely local problem (especially with the role played by federal legislation and programs in defining violations), and to be beyond the enforcement resources, capabilities, and special expertise (accountants, technical experts, program analysts and monitors, investigative specialists, and so on) of local jurisdictions and even state law-enforcement apparatus. It is within this special context then that state and local criminal-justice systems will be scrutinized.

Comprehensive Planning and Coordination

Since the advent of the Omnibus Crime Control and Safe Streets Act almost a decade ago, comprehensive criminal-justice planning, analysis, and resource allocation, organized at the state level, has been an "official" technique and policy for addressing the crime problem and a key to federal block grants to state and local jurisdictions for criminal-justice improvement. A massive planning superstructure has evolved (enjoying some $40 to $60 million annually in federal financing in the past few years) under which state planning agencies (aided by regional and local counterparts—regional planning units and criminal-justice coordinating councils) have annually produced sizeable comprehensive plans, submitted them for federal approval, and distributed federal funds in accordance with their priorities. The experience (and experiment) has not been altogether rewarding or successful. In mid-1979 the Congress and the nation were on the verge of a major crime-control-act overhaul that would place less emphasis on comprehensive written plans, probably eliminate or substantially diminish the regional and local planning superstructures, and generally place fewer federal funds into planning and more into formula and incentive grants to states and major local jurisdictions. The important point, however, is that the state planning agencies and apparatus will survive, probably under a new name, with greater state investment of dollars and with a goal of serving more as a total coordinator, rationalizer, and monitor of state criminal-justice endeavors rather than as just a conduit for federal funds.

From the very beginning, white-collar and economic crime occupied a small place in the comprehensive plans and in federal block-grant-distribution priorities. Some state plans devoted special attention to efforts in this area, but they were few. Because of the larger geographical scope and special enforcement expertise required for white-collar-crime containment, it is important that white-collar-crime-containment efforts win a place in the planning and coordination efforts to be conducted by the states under the new legislation.[11] The state planning agencies were one of the few forums where court, police, prosecution, and correctional needs and concerns were brought together, identified, ordered, and forged into a total crime-control agenda (whether viewed as a true comprehensive plan or a shopping list for federal dollars). State leadership will, it seems, be essential for effective white-collar-crime-containment programming, and while much can be supplied from and by the major state enforcement units (attorneys general, state police, bureaus of investigation), a void in the central planning/coordinating agencies that will continue to report primarily to the state governor (and his/her crime-control policy apparatus) would inevitably hurt the cause of white-collar-crime containment.

Prosecution: State and Local

The area of prosecution raises peculiar and difficult problems of coordination, leadership, and role in white-collar-crime containment. Prosecution of crimes is dominantly in the hands of the independent local (and usually elected) prosecutor. Reform groups and study commissions have for years suggested a stronger role in criminal-law enforcement on the part of the nation's attorneys general, but in only a few states is the attorney general the direct "boss" of the prosecution system and organizational supervisor of local prosecutors; and this situation shows no signs of changing. Indeed, in many states even legislative powers of attorneys general to initiate local prosecutions, intervene in local cases, or supersede local prosecutors have fallen into disuse, created much uneasiness and distrust on the part of prosecutors, and generally contributed to a gulf and lack of coordination between the state and local prosecution levels. This is unfortunate because the state attorney general often has a crucial enforcement role (albeit frequently noncriminal) in such special areas as organized crime, official corruption, consumer fraud, securities and environmental offenses (much of this either squarely within or closely linked to white-collar crime). Thus there exists a major challenge in the proper organization and coordination of white-collar-crime prosecutions below the federal level—and perhaps one of the great hurdles is the old attorney general-local prosecutor "estrangement."[12]

Nevertheless, positive forces are at work that seem to lay a groundwork for coordinated, well-orchestrated, adequately equipped efforts (even apart from federal technical aid and leadership):

1. Ten years ago the attorneys general singled out the area of consumer protection as a top-priority concern and one that should be primarily under their jurisdiction.[13] A continuing growth of staff resources, special offices, and increasing appropriations—necessary preconditions of effective white-collar-crime containment—has followed. The will is there, the precedent has been established, and the superstructure is in place, varying of course among the states but with a reasonable measure of leadership in most.

2. While the course of criminal-justice organization has not displayed any significant increase in attorney-general supervisory or policy authority over local prosecutors, a clear movement toward funded state-level technical-assistance offices to help local prosecutors perform optimally (for example, laboratory assistance, clearinghouse help, special investigators,

accountants and trial counsel, training and manual aids, and appellate research and case-law/statutory bulletins) has emerged and attracted universal acceptance. According to a 1976 survey by the NDAA, over 40 states now have such offices, most with full-time staff. Some are operated by state associations of prosecutors and some by attorney generals' offices, but even where local prosecutors sponsor broad technical-assistance programs, state attorneys general provide additional help and training in areas close to their primary responsibilities (securities frauds, consumer fraud, environmental violations, illegal insurance practices, and so on). (Another area of state attorney general responsibility is the growing and explicit role of attorneys general in enforcing federal regulatory legislation, for example, *parens patriae* authorization to recover civil damages for state consumers injured by Sherman Act antitrust violations. This seems to be a growing trend in areas other than antitrust.)

    3. As state-level criminal-justice-information systems expand and strengthen their capacities, a vehicle for adding white-collar-crime-specific data emerges. The notable effort in this area has been the LEAA-funded Project SEARCH, initiated in 1969 as a six-state prototype effort for development of offender-based criminal statistics and retrieval of criminal-history data. SEARCH now operates as a nonprofit corporation with membership composed of gubernatorial designees from all 50 states, an expanding range of operational capabilities, and an imaginative portfolio of cooperative research and demonstration projects in criminal-information-system technology.

    4. Local prosecution seems to be accepting a need for at least guidelines and principles to govern the broad discretionary scope of the independent local prosecutor. The issuance of prosecutive policies, standards, and principles enjoying some kind of uniformity among local prosecutors, even if largely consensual, will be terribly important to a maximum, coordinated, and equal-justice response to white-collar offenses. Just as important would be the facilitating of local enforcement and prosecution of matters involving concurrent federal-state jurisdiction. The criminal proscription and financial losses may be predominantly federal, but the impacts and harm are felt equally and often more dramatically at the local level. Until recently there has been too little attention given to enlisting local prosecutors for the invaluable on-site knowledge and assistance they can provide.

Police and Enforcement Structures and Issues

Policework at the state level is a "mixed bag." Nearly half the nation's state police agencies do not have general criminal law-enforcement and investigation authority but operate essentially as highway patrols. Many states have separate bureaus of investigation, with broad FBI-type investigative authority over state-law infractions. Some are within attorneys general offices, others within departments of public safety (sometimes as coequal units with uniformed state police and highway patrols), and others operate within the new (and as yet relatively rare) integrated state departments of justice. Then too in most states the attorney general holds a constitutionally independent and elected office, outside the governor's line authority. Thus with few exceptions, there is no common structural bond between state police and investigative units (under the governor) and state prosecution (under the attorney general).

This situation adds up to a tenuous police and law-enforcement leadership structure at the state level for white-collar crime enforcement, at least in most states. Major reliance will have to be placed on local (county and municipal) authorities except for investigative units directly within attorneys general offices or statewide bureaus of investigation well oriented to and integrated with attorney general consumer-protection regulatory enforcement, and white-collar-crime-containment programs.

At the local level a considerable reorientation and restructuring effort will be required for appropriate police support to white-collar-crime containment. Special investigative units focusing on white-collar crime, at least within larger police agencies, are a desirable goal (and probably a necessary technique for achieving adequate enforcement attention to white-collar-crime offenses). Also better training and orientation of line detectives and patrolmen in white-collar-crime detection and investigative roles appropriate to their day-to-day functions will be needed. With metropolitan police activity now moving toward team-policing configurations oriented to the generalist rather than the specialist and to geographical rather than substantive jurisdiction, it is important that sensitivity to the white-collar and consumer violations that threaten community and citizen safety become a part of the line officer's psyche and value system. This can be accomplished only through agency commitment, well-conceived training programs (recruit and refresher), and auxiliary and specialist services either from within the department (for large forces) or federal and state technical-assistance programs (for smaller police units and in many respects large forces as well).

The Federal Connection

The foregoing discussion raises a legitimate and important question, already touched upon, as to the appropriate federal role in stimulation of more effective state and local responses to white-collar crime. Large-scale subsidies and formula grants seem out of the question with the existing Crime Control Act Levels of investment in such aid and the mounting special-interest demands (courts, corrections, community crime prevention, and so on). Moreover, it would be difficult to target such funds, both politically and programwide, into white-collar-crime containment; and even if made available, such monies might well be diffused and diluted for general support of police, prosecution, and other enforcement operations. Yet the federal government copes daily with a broad compass of white-collar-crime problems, both geographically and in terms of kinds of offenses. Local jurisdictions (even with the state technical-assistance units) will rarely be able to support needed banks of expertise such as accountants, technical experts, health-care-program analysts, and investigative specialists required for the broad range of violations that nevertheless affect them locally. They often lack the investigative and prosecutive manpower to devote to complex cases without injuring capabilities for coping with common crimes.

Perhaps the best federal-policy direction, in most areas, would be to develop criteria and resources for provision of more support services to local enforcement agencies dealing with white-collar crime. Provision of services, especially in this complex and specialized area, is less likely to be wasteful of dollars than general financial subsidies. There are ample precedents for this in the FBI crime-laboratory services and on-line wanted-person and stolen-property [National Crime Information Center (NCIC)] computer files, in Postal Inspection Service assistance to local fraud prosecutors, and in the broad range of investigative, analytic, and advisory services provided by the SEC to local agencies enforcing state securities laws.

These federal initiatives have heretofore been a matter of federal-policy option, implemented by husbanding already limited resources for this purpose. It would not be difficult by appropriate legislation, executive order, and budgetary action to clarify the commitment and make such programs applicable to all federal agencies. This would include institutionalizing these kinds of services as line items in department and agency budgets. At relatively low cost then, broad and overlapping state- and federal-policy objectives could be better advanced, the resulting coordination would minimize the impact of "escapes" or transfer of operations from one jurisdiction to another to further victimize the public, and the message would be meaningfully conveyed that the national white-collar-crime-containment effort is a common federal-state-local problem.

Such a stance need not preclude targeted seed money or matching grants (1) to state technical-assistance agencies to add white-collar-crime-oriented services, or (2) to larger local enforcement or prosecutorial units to help establish, staff, and equip special white-collar-crime units. It also suggests that existing national training, auxiliary, and information services be reexamined to see if their white-collar-crime-containment contributions can be enhanced. For example, now that the FBI's NCIC is fully operational with terminals in all states and over 6.5 million active files (wanted persons, stolen vehicles, boats and firearms, stolen securities, computerized criminal histories, missing persons, and so on), it may be time to scrutinize this valuable service and determine what new capabilities and adjustments (perhaps minor) might increase its effectiveness as a white-collar-crime investigative tool.

The Courts

In the white-collar-crime area, courts of necessity must be "reactive" rather than "proactive" or "initiators." They must await the fruits of enforcement, investigative, and prosecutorial activities to get their "piece of the action." If prosecutions were to increase materially, the relatively complex nature of many white-collar-crime cases might create resource stresses and trial-calendar strains. The current trend toward flat or presumptive sentences will tend to reduce sentencing disparities in this field but perhaps at the cost of severity of sanction that might offer a real deterrent effect. (White-collar crimes will tend to carry light penalties in any flat-sentencing scheme that allows little discretionary leeway for the egregious offender.)

Corrections

This component of the criminal-justice system (encompassing jails, prisons, parole, probation supervision, and varied community programs) seems to have a relatively modest mission in any reshuffling of white-collar-crime-containment priorities. Correctional systems are executors of sentences and keepers and watchers of offenders. Because of the middle-class background of many white-collar offenders, the challenge here may be assuring safety to offenders who may be least able to cope with the predatory and dangerous-offender subculture of many of our jails and prisons (and, indeed, may provide balance to the increasingly younger and violent-offender element in institutional populations). For offenders under probation or parole supervision, the challenge will be different, that is, one of assuring no return to former white-collar misbehavior (which may be somewhat harder to detect in the incipient stages than street criminal activity). In short, the corrections system has little more to look forward to and plan for than a step-up in white-collar-offender personnel, which should present few special custodial problems. Appropriately severe and effective sanctions for corporate entities also require rethinking (beyond vastly increased money fines). These could include, for example, loss of permits, blacklisting, restitution to aggrieved consumers, and supervision or monitoring of postconviction behavior, but this seems more a challenge for legislatures and sentencing courts than correctional systems.[14]

State Legislative Actions

The state is the basic lawgiver and orderer of criminal administration in the United States, even at local levels. State codes define criminal activity, often regulate the basic qualifications for criminal-justice personnel, and, as we have seen, are increasingly involved in authorization of supportive and back-up roles for criminal-justice units at local levels. Since so many white-collar offenses derive from regulated activities, state codes must also see that adequate criminal sanctions are created for the various types of regulatory defaults. All this suggests that despite the heavy federal influence in deferring fraudulent and deceptive activity—whether against government, consumers, or business—an important orchestration role on the part of state legislatures is required for a concerted criminal-justice-system response. There is no harm (and often there can be enforcement benefit) in state duplication of or analogs to federal white-collar crimes if these are carefully considered and not permitted to further complicate coordinated enforcement.

Conclusion

What then does the foregoing discussion suggest in terms of criminal-justice-system adjustments and accommodations required to effectively develop, marshal, and distribute resources for white-collar-crime containment?

The system is basically "in place," and one can expect few radical changes or reprioritizations to be effected for the sake of or, perhaps more accurately, to reflect public concern with, the containment of white-collar crime. Rather, the need and the reality seem to point to more sophisticated coordination, leadership, role definition, and policy clarification in this field. As some of the manifestations of such a thrust, we can hopefully look forward to:

1. Greater federal technical assistance to state and federal components of the criminal-justice system, provided as a matter of official policy and categorized budget allocation.
2. Greater federal government coordination and rationalization of its white-collar-crime-containment activities, particularly in criminal proceedings, possibly emerging from the proposals of the president's Reor-

ganization Project for restructuring of federal law-enforcement activities and attorney legal representation.[a]

3. Assumption of a stronger state-coordinative role over the white-collar-crime-containment efforts of state, county, and municipal prosecution authorities.
4. Special-focus training of local police and investigative units from both federal and state agencies to better handle white-collar-crime-containment responsibilities and community and business relationships relative to enforcement efforts.
5. The creation of special white-collar-crime units, where not presently existent, in larger prosecution and police offices at both state and local levels.
6. Continuing research and technology utilization efforts, backed by federal crime-control funds and occasional demonstration and seed-money grant programs to validate, launch, and "prove out" promising state and local innovations.
7. State legislative backup of the foregoing arsenal of technical support, attorney general leadership, and local capabilities enhancement along with clear and forceful criminal-law-enforcement policies.
8. Development of effective information and coordination networks among state and local agencies to improve white-collar-crime-containment and particularly to meet the complex challenge of multistate schemes.

The national sense of justice has decreed, in an era of profound governmental and business corruption, of danger to public "health and welfare," of acute sensitivity to minority and class equity, and of special susceptibility to "crime by deception," that white-collar crime take its place in our hierarchy of justice-system values as a hazard comparable to common crime—perhaps a junior partner, but one worthy of a major system response. Room for such an adjustment is narrowly confined, and the system's ability to expand is equally constricted. However, the task ahead is clear, the partnership must be recognized, and the balance must be struck. Let us hope that a decade hence, some twenty years after rediscovery of the "criminal-justice system" as a system, that the white-collar-crime priority has won its place and become a meaningful part of that system's thrust.

---

[a] As of mid July 1978, reorganization options for the president's Federal Law Enforcement Study remained to be released. Initial option papers of the president's Federal Legal Representation Study (June 1978) seemed to lean toward more centralization of federal litigation authority in the Justice Department (except for regulatory litigation of the independent regulatory commissions and EEOC litigation), better coordination techniques (litigation notice system, joint or shared field-office facilities), and negotiated delegation of selected Justice litigation work to other departments and agencies.

Notes

1. Herbert Edelhertz, Ezra Stotland, Marilyn Walsh, and Milton Weinberg, *The Investigation of White-Collar Crime: A Manual for Law Enforcement Agencies* (Washington, D.C.: Government Printing Office, 1977).

2. Herbert Edelhertz, *The Nature, Impact and Prosecution of White-Collar Crime* (Washington, D.C.: Government Printing Office, 1970), pp. 73–75.

3. In terms of conviction data, the American Bar Association examines some federal statistics, for example, tax evasion, economic crime (FBI investigated), and SEC violation convictions (1,220, 3,750, and 115, respectively, in 1975). See ABA, *1978 Economic Crime Committee Informational Report;* also U.S. Attorney General, *1976 Annual Report,* pp. 20–21, 164–166, which indicates filings of 6,192 white-collar-crime cases under 12 primary categories in FY1976, approximately 15.1 percent of all federal criminal filings. These probably would be augmented substantially if we were able to thoroughly look behind statistics in more general-offense categories.

4. *U.S. Bureau of Prisons Statistical Report—1975,* tables A–9 and A–10. These white-collar-crime breakdowns include only embezzlement, fraud, income tax, and transporting false of forged securities. It is not at all clear whether all of the last category involve white-collar offenses under the definition used here; nor is it to be doubted that numerous white-collar violations are to be found in gross statistics covering larceny, counterfeiting, and forgery.

5. See Charles E. Silberman, *Criminal Violence, Criminal Justice* (New York: Random House, 1978), pp. 75–80.

6. This material on federal white-collar-crime containment draws heavily on descriptions, conclusions, and actual text offered by Herbert Edelhertz in recent congressional testimony. See 69. U.S., Congress, House, Committee on the Judiciary, Subcommittee on Crime, *White-Collar Crime,* 95th Cong., 2nd sess., 1978. See also Appendix B in this volume.

7. Office of Management and Budget, *Federal Organizations Involved in Law Enforcement, Police and Investigative Activities: Descriptive Report and Profiles,* ch. 1 (April 1978).

8. Remarks of Director William H. Webster, LEAA–National Governors' Conference "State of the Art" Workshop on Crime Control, Arlington, Virginia (31 May 1979).

9. See Assistant Attorney General James M. Moorman, Department of Justice Land and Natural Resources Division, *Criminal Enforcement of the Pollution Control Laws* (ALI–ABA Institute on Environmental Law, February 1978) (1) announcing a policy of firm criminal prosecution of will-

ful, substantial violations of pollution-control laws, (2) referring to stringent criminal penalties in federal environmental legislation and use of general false-statement and mail-fraud laws, (3) focusing on false reporting, concealment, and nonreporting in situations of substantial harm or danger, and (4) viewing criminal enforcement as a conscious tool to put teeth into self-policing programs.

10. See, for example, LEAA funding of the NDAA's Economic Crime Project aggregating over $3 million from 1973 through 1978 (current grant #78–DF–AX–0170) to assist local prosecutors' offices in launching special units, increasing general white-collar-crime-containment capabilities, and enhancing public and community awareness; other examples include the LEAA-supported development of a manual, *The Investigation of White-Collar Crime,* and the establishing of the National Center on White-collar Crime at Battelle.

11. See S. 3270, Justice System Improvement Act of 1978. The proposed new agencies are "Criminal Justice Councils" at the state level, and "Criminal Justice Advisory Boards" for major local units.

12. One positive side of attorney general–local prosecutor separateness is the check-and-balance impact this provides over local-government corruption. Neither state nor local officials are immune from white-collar-criminal behavior, including enforcement personnel. Indeed, if U.S. Justice Department reports are correct, enforcement in this area is a "growth industry." See *1976 Annual Report of the Attorney General of the U.S.,* pp. 7–8.

13. National Association of Attorneys General, *The Office of the Attorney General,* part 6.6 (1971), and *Powers, Duties and Operations of State Attorneys General,* parts II.10 and V.26 (October 1977).

14. See, in this regard, enhanced money fines, stronger collection authority, and provisions for restitution and notice of conviction to victims under the proposed new Federal Criminal Code (S. 1437 and H.R. 6869).

6 The Criminal-Justice-System Challenge of White-Collar Crime

Mary V. McGuire

The second part of this volume focuses primarily on the role that has been played by the criminal-justice system in its efforts to contain white-collar crime. Secondarily, that section explores the role that the criminal-justice system *should* play in establishing policy for containment of and in enforcing white-collar crime. As Daniel Skoler (and others) pointed out, the approach taken by the criminal-justice system in the past has involved far too little policy and has been encumbered by the decentralized nature of the criminal-justice system, which focuses the vast majority of its energies at state and local levels. Furthermore, the treatment of white-collar crime has suffered from being placed in a position of relatively low priority within the system, which, of course, must divide its limited resources among the gamut of criminal activity.

Any discussion of the actual and potential scope of the criminal-justice system's white-collar-crime-containment efforts necessarily includes consideration of three factors: (1) communication and coordination within and among the various levels of the criminal-justice system; (2) links between the criminal-justice system and other systems of justice; and (3) the utilization by the criminal-justice system of all available resources in its efforts to enforce white-collar-crime laws. Accordingly, attention has been given in this volume to intrasystem, intersystem, and extrasystem functioning and capabilities.

The Nature of the Challenge

It is difficult at the present time, if not impossible, to ascertain the scope of white-collar crime in the United States. Although law enforcement has the technology for extensive data collection and compilation, the technology has not yet been applied to the area of white-collar crime. Hence though definitions of white-collar crime have been proposed, the precise nature and extent of the crime area remain somewhat amorphous. It is apparently easier to define white-collar crime than it is to characterize it.

Despite the difficulties of clearly detailing its nature and extent, white-collar crime does present challenges and problems to all levels of the criminal-justice system: white-collar crime is not a problem confined to the federal level, contrary to some popular notions of the problem. All levels of the criminal-justice system (federal, state, and local) have the authority to engage in the enforcement of white-collar crime, and as Skoler so clearly illustrates in his paper, the vast majority of criminal-justice system activity is carried on at state and local levels. While there may be a trend toward greater centralization within the criminal-justice system, no sound policy for white-collar-crime containment has been articulated at the federal level or elsewhere. Hence the state and local levels of the criminal-justice system address their white-collar-crime-containment responsibilities armed with the bulk of the criminal-justice system's resources but without a comprehensive strategy. Just as the criminal-justice system has been termed a "nonsystem," the approach taken by the criminal-justice system to white-collar-crime containment might be considered a "nonapproach."

White-Collar-Crime Containment at the Federal Level

The flaw of the criminal-justice system's approach to white-collar-crime at the federal level is that of having failed to articulate either a policy for white-collar-crime containment or a policy for communication and effective coordination within the criminal-justice system, with other systems of justice (civil or administrative), and with the private sector. (However, current Justice Department objectives now include priority attention to the development of such policies.) While there is no question that the federal level is not presently equipped to handle great increases in direct detection, investigation, and prosecution of white-collar crimes, the federal level *can* assume increased back-up and leadership responsibilities by articulating a system-wide policy for white-collar-crime containment. This would almost certainly increase the effectiveness of white-collar-crime containment.

In the absence of a solid federal policy for white-collar-crime containment, it is not surprising that the separation of jurisdictions at the federal level, as well as the vertical separation of powers within the criminal-justice system, have created serious problems for white-collar-crime containment. At the federal level, criminal, civil, and administrative jurisdictions may be asserted to enforce white-collar crime. The nature of the offender, or the nature of the offense, may well suggest that the maximally effective jurisdiction for enforcement lies outside the criminal-justice system; however, only rarely has effective exchange occurred between the criminal-justice system and either the civil justice system or administrative agencies. Relevent here is not only the question of the most appropriate place to assert jurisdiction, but also the question of the effective use of resources. Often, valuable expertise lies within a particular governmental agency or even within the private sector; when the criminal-justice system fails to work effectively with such experts, an unfortunate underutilization of available resources results. An effective policy for intersystem coordination could greatly alleviate such problems.

Just as questions arise concerning the appropriate place to assert jurisdiction and the effective utilization of skills and resources between the criminal-justice system and other systems of justice, comparable questions arise within the criminal-justice system itself. Since it is, currently at any rate, not feasible for the federal government to handle all criminal-justice-system activity related to the containment of white-collar crime and since the majority of criminal-justice-system activity is carried out at state and local levels, a systemwide policy for white-collar-crime containment and for intrasystem coordination is badly needed. This policy should include guidelines for allocating responsibilities where there is concurrent jurisdiction and for sharing resources. While the most appropriate criteria for determining the level at which jurisdiction should be asserted could be determined only through careful policy analysis, several issues may well come into play here. For example, geographical considerations suggest one natural means for guiding the assertion of jurisdiction and hence the direct involvement of different levels of the criminal-justice system in white-collar-crime containment; the federal level of the criminal-justice system may be in a better position to handle multistate white-collar-crime cases than is either the state or local level. Type of offense, the offender, the victim, or the scope of the impact of a particular white-collar crime might also dictate the appropriate level within the criminal-justice system at which jurisdiction should be asserted. Additionally, consideration of the means by which all resources available to the criminal-justice system may be most effectively brought to bear may well suggest guidelines for asserting jurisdiction. State and local levels of the criminal-justice system may be in better positions to utilize some private-sector resources than the federal level. Thus a systemwide policy is called for that creates effective mechanisms for coordination of activities within the criminal-justice system and for utilization of all available resources.

Implicit in this federal role of policy setting is a federal role of leadership and back-up for other levels of the criminal-justice system. The indirect support provided by the federal level for the entire criminal-justice system can and should be supplemented with technical training, information dissemination, and record-keeping. Additionally, the statement of federal policy for white-collar-crime containment (1) should include a clear statement of the extent to which the federal level is and will be directly involved in white-collar-crime containment and (2) should provide guidelines for federal subsidization (actual monetary support) for activities and specialized programs at state and local levels.

White-Collar-Crime Enforcement at the State and Local Levels

Many state attorneys general have no criminal jurisdiction while many local prosecutors and district attorneys have no authority to assert civil jurisdiction in investigating, prosecuting, or enforcing laws against white-collar-crime offenses. Thus cooperation within the criminal-justice system often requires cooperation among different justice systems. As such, the importance of effective federal-state-local cooperation within the criminal-justice system *and* cooperation among criminal, civil, and administrative systems of justice are underscored at state and local levels.

In a number of instances, effective communication and cooperation has been established within the criminal-justice system and among different justice systems. There are several examples of this cooperation: A council was established and effectively implemented in Texas to facilitate federal-state cooperation in the enforcement of white-collar crime; federal-local cooperation has been successfully accomplished through the cross-deputization of assistant district attorneys and U.S. attorneys in New Jersey (this has since taken place in Wisconsin and California); and profitable federal-local interaction was achieved through cooperation on individual cases between the SEC and the King County Prosecutor's Office in Seattle, Washington. Such instances of cooperation serve as evidence of the merits of coordinating enforcement efforts, the feasibility of sharing resources, and the potential for increased effectiveness of white-collar-crime containment. Unfortunately, this sort of cooperation often occurs in isolation and lacks the solid underpinnings federal leadership, back-up, and policy could offer. In short, such cooperation has not really been institutionalized or formalized but has an ad-hoc character. Thus illustrations of unhappy failures in attempts to coordinate activities are found along with illustrations of successes.

Comments on "The Criminal-Justice-System Challenge"

The second section of this volume does not directly address the task of constructing a national strategy for white-collar-crime containment, though it does begin to analyze prospectively the strategies, tactics, and barriers involved in the development of a national strategy. In focusing on the role of the criminal-justice system in containing white-collar crime, this chapter provides an opportunity for discussion of current and past approaches to white-collar crime. Furthermore, the chapter succeeds in raising a number of issues, procedural and substantive, that are relevant and perhaps essential to mapping a strategy for white-collar-crime containment.

First, clearly illustrated is the difficulty of the task of developing a strategy for white-collar-crime containment. As with the development of any strategy, it is easy to fall prey to the desire, and need, to criticize or praise existing programs while losing sight of the ultimate goal of strategy development. One cannot give in to the tendency to slip into discussions that involve defending one's own turf when faced with the complex task of projecting future strategy. Thus one should bear in mind the procedural difficulties of strategy development and the urgency of transcending individual agency jurisdictional considerations in order to achieve the goal of developing and implementing an effective, efficient, prospective strategy.

However, analyzing the strengths and weaknesses of the criminal-justice system's present approach to white-collar-crime containment, or the state of the art of white-collar-crime containment efforts, serves as a starting point for strategy development. This process focuses attention on several substantive factors and considerations that should be addressed in a national strategy for white-collar-crime containment. While these factors and considerations are discussed previously, they merit emphasis and are summarized below.

1. *Articulation of federal policy:* There is great need for the development of an explicit federal policy for white-collar-crime containment. This policy must detail the position and responsibilities of the federal level of the criminal-justice system and provide for federal back-up, leadership, information dissemination, and training for all elements of the criminal-justice system. Guidelines should be provided for effective detection, investigation, prosecution, and treatment of offenders, as well as for allocation of jurisdictional responsibilities among and utilization of resources by the various levels of government.

2. *Federal-state-local coordination within the criminal-justice system:* To develop an effective approach for containing white-collar crime, all facets of the criminal-justice system must be able to coordinate activities, share resources, and cooperate in every way possible. Such systemwide coordination requires strong federal back-up and leadership, as well as direct federal involvement in enforcement activities. However, the federal government should not dominate white-collar-crime containment efforts. Federal, state, and local governments must be full partners in the process of white-collar-crime containment; allocations of responsibilities and utilization of resources must reflect rational and objective criteria designed to most effectively meet the challenges of white-collar-crime containment.

3. *Criminal-, civil-, and administrative-justice-systems coordination:* To develop a maximally effective policy for white-collar-crime containment, the criminal-justice system must not work in isolation but should establish effective links with other justice systems at federal, state, and local

levels to facilitate efficient and appropriate assertion of jurisdiction, imposition of sanctions, and utilization of available remedies and resources. Again strong back-up and leadership functions at the federal level could greatly enhance such functioning.

4. *Facilitating community relations:* A national strategy for white-collar-crime containment should also provide for links between public and private sectors to ensure that all resources and support available to the criminal-justice system are effectively utilized. All levels of the criminal-justice system stand to benefit from the expertise and interest of the private sector. Appropriate, effective links to the private sector not only enable the criminal-justice system to utilize valuable resources, but may also facilitate and create incentives for further cooperation between the private and public sectors in efforts to contain white-collar crime.

Part IV
National Strategy of Development and Implementation

7

Developing a Strategy to Contain White-Collar Crime

William A. Morrill

This chapter has been prepared to provoke discussion on developing a white-collar-crime-containment strategy not from the perspective of expertise in the substance of the subject matter but rather from the more general perspective of developing strategies about social problems and issues that appear to dictate collective action by the society. While the expertise in white-collar crime is indispensable to the evolution of a strategy, the more general perspective may contribute both insight and experience to the development of a strategy through shared characteristics.

The common ground shared by a large number of social problems and issues in the United States that calls forth a societal response—usually through governmental institutions—can be expressed as follows: When the behavior of some in the society imposes heavy costs expressed in dollar or other terms, denies deserved opportunities, confers unwarranted benefits, and such behavior cannot be appropriately dealt with by individuals, then collective action by the society is often undertaken through governments to relieve such imposition of costs, equalize opportunity, or rearrange the conferring of benefits. Such societal action may take the form of:

Regulation, used here in its broadest meaning to include statutes, rule making, mandatory professional standards, and other promulgations that establish enforceable affirmative duties or prohibit behavior or both (specifically including the criminal-justice system).

Establishment of *incentives* such as tax credits for certain actions.

Conferring of *benefits* through public expenditures such as programs for the disadvantaged.

Provision of *information and education* such as some consumer-protection laws.

The selection of one or some combination of these forms of societal action is often dictated by the nature of the issue, though it is sometimes surprising

The author would like to acknowledge the helpful contribution of ideas and comments of his MPR colleague, Christy Schmidt, in the preparation of this chapter.

how little thought or discussion is given to the selection of the four or even recognition that there may be a choice to be made. The traditions of this country have been to limit societal intervention through government to those clearly public goods and services or circumstances in which individual or private-sector transactions produce unacceptable results, and then only to the extent needed to correct the perceived problem. Though this tradition has been subject to stress and strain in the face of an increasingly complex and interdependent society, we are still very much a mixed public-private economy and nation with continuing skepticism of government.

The development of strategy for societal action about social issues and problems—or at least successful ones—likewise appears to have some desirable common elements independent of particulars of the issue involved. While these elements may vary in shape, duration, and importance, they may be useful as at least a model from which one can depart. These elements in a logical order, though not necessarily in precise sequence of occurrence, would include the following:

1. A *substantive analytic* element designed to illuminate the nature of the problem being addressed; to identify and examine the possible courses of societal action including nonaction; and to select or establish a process for selecting the best available course of action.

While this all seems straightforward enough, it in fact is not that easy as witnessed by a landscape populated with an uncomfortable number of mid-diagnosed problems, dysfunctional programs and instances where we employed an elephant gun to slay a gnat or a gnat to slay an elephant (for example, a direct federal program to supervise youth-camp safety on the one hand, and only 150 federal people assigned in 1975 to supervise the Medicaid program of about $14 billion in 1975 on the other). This element is closely coupled to the next.

2. An *institutional- and process-assessment* element designed to evaluate the adequacy of existing institutions and processes for carrying out the societal action selected; to determine whether new institutions and new or revised processes may be needed to carry out the strategy; and to devise some plan for ensuring that there are effective institutions and processes through which the conclusions reached in the substantive analytic element can be implemented.

If the United States has been periodically haphazard in its coping with the substantive analytic effort, its performance on the institutional- and process-assessment element reflects a much larger calamity. In our zeal to solve substantive social problems, we have all too often varied between glorious indifference to the importance of institutional and process considerations and the continual creation of new and untried institutions and processes with equally bad results. One need not be an expert in institutional behavior to know that institutions—particularly complex ones—in which people work and processes through which things happen can make a powerful if not overwhelming impact on outcomes—for good or ill. If one does not arrange effectively for how and through whom an effort is going to be made, not much is likely to happen given institutional inertia.

3. A *relatively rigorous experiment or demonstration* element designed to test in the "real world" the conclusions reached in the preceding elements; to remove or narrow the remaining uncertainties; and to develop convincing evidence of the probable effectiveness, replicability and indirect outcomes of the one or more substantive, institutional and process measures selected.

This element is not always appropriate or possible for technical or timing reasons, but it does commend itself on several grounds. Experience suggests that even the best of plans concocted in offices may produce unanticipated and unintended consequences when implemented in the messy real world. Experiments or demonstrations, if carefully done, narrow the potential for future operational failure and sometimes produce unexpected knowledge and benefits. In addition, when the analytic results suggest a course of action that is counterintuitive or that touches deeply rooted values and emotions, the experiment or demonstration—indeed a number of them on related topics—may be useful and necessary to help quell fears (for example, the role of the income-maintenance experiments in reducing the fear that support of two-parent families would cause massive withdrawal from the labor force). Finally, the rigorous experiment or demonstration produces not only a useful body of empirical evidence, it also develops a group of knowledgeable people who will in turn help generate public discussion and support.

A few words of caution are in order about the use of this element. If it is to be useful at all, it must be done with enough care and precision so that the consequences of the new action are separated from all other effects and that effects are properly measured. This dictum is sometimes methodologically impossible and usually not easy. Such efforts are also relatively expensive due to design, data-collection, and analysis costs, and they are relatively long-term due to the time required to observe results. As such, this element may not always be practical or appropriate and should be undertaken only where important issues cannot be resolved objectively or politically with available evidence and where the potential pay-off is high. While this element in developing a strategy may be optional, the next one is not.

4. An *education and consensus-building* element designed to consult *all* important actors and constituencies *during* the construction of the strategy and before decisions are made; bring important evidence and ideas to the attention of expert, special, and general publics; and be open to ideas, compromise, and alternative views throughout the process.

The notion of consensus building is hardly novel; however, it now has a new dimension. In a post-Watergate environment, which heightened an already deepening suspicion of large institutions of all kinds, the days in which a relatively few well-placed people could devise, establish, and implement a strategy on a major social issue and *then* worry about consensus building are about gone. A new approach is needed.

In the past it was common in the development of a national strategy to consult experts, friends, and a few key leaders in the executive branch, Congress, and powerful private individuals and usually *avoid* individuals or constituencies suspected of being or actually in opposition; information supporting the desired strategy would be arrayed and contraevidence and views buried. Experience suggests that this approach will not work much any more, whereas an open, inclusive process—albeit somewhat frustrating—will. For example, after 18 months of rancor and impasse among the executive branch, Congress, the states, and more than 100 different interest groups, the Congress in the fall of 1975 enacted a major new title to the Social Security Act prescribing a multibillion-dollar social-services program. The final hearings and debate for this bill, however, were measured in hours. This somewhat unusual event occurred only because of a laborious but productive six months of open consultation with all interested parties to hammer out a consensus statute. By contrast, one can find many strategies developed through closed processes that came apart in the legislature or in implementation for lack of adequate consensus building. Although usually not considered a part of the development of a strategy, the final element, evaluation, is in fact an important part of the picture.

5. An *evaluation* element designed to articulate in advance the measures by which the strategy can be judged to be progressing satisfactorily or have succeeded; set up the system to collect the information needed to apply the measures; and force decision making when the results achieved vary from the intended.

While it is often though that this uncomfortable element can be delayed until after the strategy is launched, such delay can be fatal to both useful evaluation and effective results later. If collection of information about measures of success occurs after the strategy is in progress, it may be impossible to reconstruct the place from which one started (the baseline). Further, thinking through the measures by which the strategy should be judged *in advance* tends to sharpen the objectives of the strategy and add a healthy dose of realism to the expectations. While strategies with panacea promises are politically appealing, they unfortunately have a day of reckoning in subsequent disillusionment, faltering support, and inadequate results.

It is obvious that these elements of developing a successful strategy are somewhat idealized since those who are concerned with strategy development rarely find themselves starting with a clean slate and must enter the "play" somewhere in "Act II" after a good many events about the issue have already occurred. Nonetheless, these general notion about societal action and the desirable elements of strategy development may provide a useful framework within which to consider the evolution of a white-collar-crime-containment strategy—to see how these general concepts might or might not apply.

This application necessarily starts with consideration of the special characteristics of the white-collar-crime issue that distinguish it from other problems or present important issues in strategy development (other chapters have dealt more comprehensively with the white-collar-crime problem). To the nonexpert eye, some of the special or important characteristics of significance to the development of a white-collar-crime-containment strategy would include the following.

1. *There is fuzziness in the definition of white-collar crime.* By this, I do not mean the effort and debate to establish a mutually exclusive category of activities or persons that constitute white-collar crime or criminals. That debate—however interesting and important—has progressed at least far enough to provide a working definition for strategy development, and this kind of definitional fuzziness is not uncommon in other social issues, for example, the definition of *poverty.* The fuzziness that is striking in this context is the thin line between what is illegal, what is unethical but legal, and what is considered legitimate "beating" or taking advantage of the "system." Further, recent history and current trends would suggest that activities now not illegal but merely unethical or legitimate "game" playing may be made illegal by statute or other regulatory action.

This fuzziness has very large implications for strategy, particularly in the substantive and consensus-building elements. For example, the public may remain unaroused by and unsupportive of enforcement programs designed to contain behavior that they have difficulty perceiving as improper and that may only recently have been declared illegal.

2. A second characteristic of white-collar crime of apparent significance to a containment strategy is *the heterogeneity of the motivations for and perpetrators of such acts, further complicated by differing knowledge and motives among victims.* As Jameson Doig and Douglas Phillips have noted,[1] the motivations for white-collar crimes are not only for personal advantage but also for furtherance of organizational goals where personal reward may be seen as indirect at most. Likewise, the perpetrators of white-collar crimes may be single or a small group of individuals, large numbers of officials in otherwise legitimate organizations, or organizations whose primary purposes are the conduct of illegal activities. To make matters yet

worse, the victims of the crime may be wholly unaware of their victimization (for example, collusive price fixing) or if they are aware, may have strong incentives not to report their victimization.

This kind of heterogeneity has enormous implications for the substance of a strategy and the institutional and process mechanisms employed to pursue it. A desired and sought-after characteristic of a strategy is conceptual consistency throughout; our sense of logic and neatness tends to demand it. Yet the heterogeneity of the problem may dictate otherwise. In the quite different field of welfare policy, the logic of equitable treatment of individuals and families with little or no income and the desirable goal of a simple and manageable system drive one in the direction of a common set of cash grants based on income and family size. But the heterogeneity of the special income needs of some individuals (for example, the roof blows off in a wind storm and there are no savings to pay for a new one) forces one to a subset strategy (that is, an emergency-needs program) that is conceptually inconsistent with the basic program.

In white-collar crime, one can visualize a part of the strategy in the prevention and detection area as including measures to strengthen internal organizational monitoring and control to deter such activity. While this step could be beneficial in most cases, it obviously will not work where the entire organization is involved in the perpetration of the crime.

3. *A third striking characteristic of white-collar crime is the uncertainty of its scope and the potential for the future.* As in the case of the definition, the wide range of the estimated incidence is not a problem per se since the lower bound of the estimates is still large enough to warrant societal action (though it is always somewhat unnerving when the range between the lower and upper bounds is a great deal larger than the absolute value of the lower bound).

What is important about the uncertainty are two strong implications for strategy development. First, the uncertainty points to the great importance of detection activities in a white-collar-crime-containment strategy. Second, a wide range of estimates strongly implies a strategy that seeks to probe and narrow that range. In other words, instead of more general data collection, perhaps the strategy should comprise a sequential set of experimental steps in some of the better targets of opportunity designed to detect, prevent, or prosecute white-collar crimes. Said differently, one might structure some selected efforts to figure out how much is going on and how to get at it, refining the estimates of the total universe as a by-product as well as limiting resource commitments until after the approach proved workable. With respect to the future prospects of white-collar crime, it would appear that the trends toward an increasingly complex, technological, and specialized society have widened the opportunities for and increased the problems in detecting white-collar crime. Further, there is little reason to expect this trend to abate in the foreseeable future.

Computer crimes provide a lively example. The already existing complexity and specialization and the potential for future growth also have strong implications for the substantive, institutional, and process dimensions of a white-collar crime strategy. For example, if the nature of the detection issue alone did not drive the strategy to inclusion of noncriminal justice as well as criminal-justice agencies as substantial actors in the implementation of substantive actions, the specialization, complexity, and technological dimension of the society and the probable growth therein surely would. It would seem wholly unrealistic to expect that either the resources for or ability to recruit the skilled expertise could reasonably keep pace with the expanded potential for white-collar crime; and indeed, the mindless addition of investigative and prosecutorial resources to the criminal-justice system—even if possible—appears unlikely to be cost effective.

4. *A fourth and related characteristic of the white-collar-crime problem of apparent importance to the development of a strategy is the very large number of organizations and institutions already involved in the issue that have conflicting goals, motivations, traditions, and limitations.* Further, this universe is likely to grow rather than diminish. In the explicating this point, it should be emphasized and understood that the conflict among goals is not conflict among some goals with merit and other without but rather a conflict of goals, all of which have merit.

It is or should be increasingly recognized that one has to trade off between desirable goals. The federal student-loan and grant programs, which have been the subject of recent attention because of substantial fraud and abuse, provide a convenient example. It is quite possible to conceive of a guaranteed-student-loan program that would severely limit the potential for abuse by substantially tightening the rules by which banks can make guaranteed loans. While such actions would, without doubt, reduce default rates, it would with equal certainty reduce the chances that the lower-income students that the program is most trying to help would get loans at all. This is not to suggest that efforts to reduce abuse of student-aid programs are inappropriate but that there are clear trade-offs to be made between a valid abuse-reduction objective and an equally valid objective to improve the access of low-income persons to postsecondary education.

Motivational conflict among concerned institutions is of a similar variety. To extend the previous example, the Department of Justice sees itself as an investigator and prosecutor of those who defraud government programs, while the Department of Health, Education and Welfare generally perceives itself to be in the business of helping poor people. Conflicting traditions present some exceedingly troublesome issues. Legal theory, if not its practice, and the traditional notions of accountability for public funds assume an absolute standard—either you have committed an illegal act or you have not, or you have spent a public dollar properly or you have not. By contrast, any administrator of a complex program such as the federal social insurance and welfare program knows that the very complexity of the undertaking makes 100 percent accountability and zero-percent error, abuse and fraud an impossible dream. This situation raises an uncomfortable trade-off concerning how much abuse and fraud is tolerable.

Finally, institutions face all sorts of limitations that increase institutional conflicts including lack of resources, inability to recruit talented persons for what may be seen as secondary missions and inability to share information under privacy legislation. The large number of organizations together with understandable conflict have of course a huge impact on the development of strategy, particularly the institutional and process element. While one might with otherwise, there appears to be no magic solution to these issues. Under these circumstances, the impulse to "reorganize" in some fashion is often overwhelming. Experience suggests, however, that "reorganizations," while a potentially useful tool, rarely make underlying substantive and process problems go away. What is likely to be a more productive approach in the longer run is to deal candidly and sensitively with these conflicts and attempt to evolve one or more successful and innovative models of effective institutional interaction and cooperation which can then be more widely adopted.

5. A fifth and also interconnected characteristic of the white-collar-crime problem of importance to a strategy is a special problem of societal reaction to large organizations. The public frustration or anger with being ripped off or manhandled by large organizations of all kinds is apparent, and efforts to limit the knowledge and power of such institutions has taken tangible expression in the form of privacy and freedom-of-information legislation of various kinds. In the process of curing one problem, however, such legislation greatly complicates the detection and prosecution of white-collar crimes. To return to a prior example, the detection of abuse and fraud in the federal student-aid programs could be strengthened by HEW access to individual federal tax returns; however, such access raises serious issues under the Federal Privacy Act. It seems both unlikely and undesirable that privacy legislation will or should be eliminated or seriously eroded; therefore, a white-collar-crime-containment strategy will need to be fashioned with great sensitivity and creativeness to these issues if needed public support is to be maintained.

Having described important characteristics of the white-collar-crime problem to the development of a containment strategy and drawn at least some of the implications of those characteristics for the desirable elements of any strategy, it is perhaps useful to advance some of the general and specific features of a white-collar-crime-containment strategy that this analysis suggests. After advancing a few general points, it seems convenient and probably more familiar to do so within the more usual categorizations used in the criminal-justice system—prevention, detection, prosecution, and penalties.

General. The analysis suggests one almost overwhelming conclusion— namely, that there is no way to mount an effective strategy to contain white-collar crime within the framework of the criminal-justice agencies alone. The problems, issues, and needs in prevention, detection, and consensus building all dictate a more broadly based strategy and would foredoom a more narrowly based effort to failure. It appears desirable to include not only those public and private institutions whose activities may be most open to white-collar crimes but also some less obvious organizations who may be able to make a contribution to prevention and detection activities such as consumer organizations in connection with illegal price fixing. Also it would seem to go without saying that some careful linking of federal, state, and local criminal-justice-agency resources would be an indispensable part of the strategy.

A second general point arising from the analysis would be that some heavy analytic effort is needed in the development of a strategy, particularly with respect to the trade-offs among competing goals and objectives and maintaining the proper incentives and disincentives to discourage illegal acts. A third general conclusion is the size and importance of the consensus-building task due to the special characteristics of the problem, which would seem to dictate a very substantial effort throughout the development of the strategy and in implementation. These same characteristics would also seem to dictate that careful distinctions be made in this effort between informing and preaching and between leading and being ''way ahead of the pack.''

Prevention and detection. Any successful strategy to contain white-collar crime must contain both strong and effective prevention and detection measures in order to limit its spread. It also seems likely that the systems, activities, and programs that are inviting targets for white-collar crime may be more vulnerable to such crime than needs to be the case by virtue of lack of expertise, concentration on other goals or just indifference. Some operators of such activities and programs may also lack skills in monitoring their undertakings for possible illegal activity.

This suggests two possible specific components of a strategy. With respect to public programs, a strong effort could be made to reduce to acceptable levels the vulnerability of public programs that might include technical assistance from the criminal-justice agencies in ways to limit vulnerabilities and a mandatory review, perhaps again by the criminal-justice agencies, of all major programs and systems subject to abuse to ensure that unnecessary vulnerabilities have been eliminated. A second component involving both public and private programs or activities might be several experimental and collaborative efforts between criminal justice and non-criminal organizations to explore innovative approaches to improved detection of white-collar crime.

Prosecution and penalties. Much is made in the literature about the effort and difficulty in developing prosecutable cases, the inclination to use noncriminal remedies and the problems for prosecutors created by the complexity and technicalities of the substance of the cases. This set of problems clearly suggests some careful thinking about institutional barriers and roles and perhaps calls for some selected experimental efforts between criminal justice and non-criminal-justice agencies starting early in the detection phase to try adjustments to institutional roles in order to determine whether more effective solutions to these problems can be reached.

Much is also made in the literature about the disparity of sanctions for persons convicted of white-collar crime and those convicted of street crimes. Beyond the causalities arising from differing societal views about the seriousness of the two kinds of crime, part of the differential may also arise from perceptions of the culpability of organizational leaders for acts committed by their employees. In developing an effective sanction component to a strategy, the responsibility of organizational leadership for acts committed by employees for furtherance of organizational goals should be carefully rethought.

These preliminary specific suggestions clearly need further consideration, and there will be—no doubt—many other specific ideas meriting examination. Those offered here illustrate the kinds of actions that will tend to emerge from the careful development of a national strategy. As noted earlier, the development of a strategy is an iterative process. The elements described in the initial framework for a strategy need to be developed and then reexamined to ensure that each part is sensible in relationship to the others. The general framework can provide a checklist role as the strategy evolves. It helps to make the development of a strategy manageable. With a problem as heterogeneous and sizeable as white-collar crime, it is tempting to conclude that the problem is too large and complex for any concerted action or to concentrate on a narrow dimension of the problem. This analysis suggests that neither of these choices is necessary or desirable.

Note

1. Jameson W. Doig and Douglas E. Phillips, "Deterring Illegal Behavior by Officials of Complex Organizations," 1978 (draft).

8

Meeting the Challenge of White-Collar Crime: Evolving a National Strategy

Frederic A. Morris

Obviously, the two-day symposium that is the basis for this book could not purport to develop a comprehensive national strategy for white-collar-crime containment, even in broad outline. Indeed, each chapter of this book serves to drive home the extraordinarily complex analytic, institutional, and political issues that such an effort will involve. Against this backdrop, the third part addressed the more limited preliminary problem: How to go about evolving such a strategy. This problem raises two basic questions: What sort of effort is required and who should undertake it?

Background

William A. Morrill grappled with the first question in chapter 7 "Developing a Strategy to Contain White-Collar Crime" and in his opening remarks. In Morrill's view, government may respond to social problems such as white-collar crime in four distinct ways: by imposing regulations, by establishing incentives, by conferring benefits, or by providing information and education. Of course, these responses are not mutually exclusive. The most effective social strategies often employ an imaginative combination of responses from several categories. Any effort to evolve a national strategy for containing white-collar crime should devote considerable energy to exploring this full range of response in devising alternatives. Overlooking major response categories could represent a significant loss of opportunity.

The task of devising a strategy from responses within each category involves five basic elements: (1) a substantive analytic element, (2) an institutional and process element, (3) an experiment or demonstration element, (4) an education and consensus-building element, and (5) an evaluation element. These elements should be mutually supporting. For example, the demonstration should lend itself to evaluation. Or, to take another example, institutional arrangements should be designed to help build consensus. To design a strategy in which the various elements complement each other, the five elements should not be tackled in a simple once-through sequence. Evolution of a well-developed strategy will require repeated consideration of all the elements in an iterative process.

Morrill drew several implications from the nature of the white-collar-crime problem for application of this "recipe" to development of a national strategy.

The first implication stems from the difficulty of applying criminal proscriptions to specific fact patterns in the white-collar-crime area. The relevant statute or regulation rarely provides a bright line for distinguishing illegal activities from practices that are dubious but legal. As a result, the public may be unsure of which kinds of conduct are or should be illegal. This fact could stand in the way of building a consensus about what abuses a national strategy should target. In coping with this dilemma, those involved in developing a national strategy should exploit the analytic element to support the consensus-building element. They should develop coherent and convincing rationales for concentrating on particular areas of abuse.

The second implication—amply illustrated by the discussion of Mark Moore's typology in chapter 3—arises from the disconcertingly complex mix of motives, offenders, and victims encompassed by white-collar crime. To address this complexity, the strategy that emerges will likely have to be multitiered. Despite the natural desire for consistency, a single logic may be incapable of supporting a strategy that deals with the full array of white-collar crimes.

The third implication results from the great uncertainty about the present scope of white-collar-crime activity and its economic and social consequences. Development of a national strategy should include development of the information needed to reduce this uncertainty. Better information would serve two purposes. First, it would help indicate the level of social resources appropriate for combatting white-collar crime. Second, it would help enlist support for the enterprise. People probably now underestimate the scope of white-collar crime. In all likelihood, the relative invisibility of white-collar crime accounts for its low public and official priority. But there is enough uncertainty that it would be imprudent simply to assert that white-collar crime is a "big problem." Overestimating the scope of white-collar crime could be as self-defeating as underestimating it. Such a mistake could improperly drain resources away from other important social problems. And it could lead public support to turn to apathy or even hostility when the actual figures became known. Accordingly, any national strategy should strive to narrow this range of uncertainty early in the effort.

The fourth implication stems from the large number of institutions with conflicting goals already participating in the task of containing white-collar crime. A national strategy should address the institutional issues of white-collar-crime containment without mistakenly equating institutional fragmentation with the totality of the problem. In the face of substantive ignorance there is a great temptation simply to reorganize. This temptation should be vigorously resisted. Unless careful analysis precedes reorganization, the immediate results will inevitably be meager and the possibility of useful reform postponed.

Finally, Morrill advanced several features of a white-collar-crime-containment strategy tentatively suggested by his preliminary analysis.

First, the issues are so complicated and the need for widespread support and cooperation so great that the analytic element (especially as applied to conflicting institutional goals) and the consensus-building element merit particular emphasis.

Second, a workable strategy probably cannot rely on the criminal-justice system alone. This conclusion rests partly on the observation that the criminal-justice system is poorly positioned to detect many types of white-collar abuses at acceptable cost and with tolerable intrusions on day-to-day business and governmental activities. Since participants in the criminal-justice system are likely to exert a strong influence in the formulation of a national strategy, they must prepare themselves to assign key roles to others in implementing the strategy. Imaginatively engaging a variety of institutions is more important than worrying about who will get the credit.

Third, in distributing the responsibility of white-collar-crime control, the criminal-justice system can make a major contribution by helping the victims of white-collar crime become less vulnerable to abuse. In particular, the criminal-justice system can help institutional victims design internal procedures and social programs that are more resistant to abuse and more capable of detecting illicit activities when they occur.

Fourth, the criminal-justice system may be able to help victims and other institutions outside the criminal-justice system in detecting white-collar abuses and dealing with offenders.

Morrill's chapter evokes two questions: First, what sort of effort is needed? In particular, what are the appropriate goals of a national strategy? What is the role of evaluation? What are the inadequacies of current institutional structures and relationships? How can educative or consensus-building programs contribute? Second, who should manage the effort and perform the analysis?

Appropriate Goals for a White-Collar-Crime-Containment Strategy

Means cannot be devised or evaluated without reference to some agreed upon ends. Therefore development of a national strategy requires some initial agreement on what the goals of the effort should be. In developing goals, several important issues arise.

A preliminary consideration in setting goals for a national strategy stems from the recognition that the objective of containing white-collar crime may sometimes conflict with other important and legitimate social goals. For example, the fundamental goal of a guaranteed-student-loan program—getting money into the hands of needy students—may conflict with the goal of limiting fraud by ineligible recipients. Other social-welfare programs pose analogous dilemmas. An early priority in developing a national strategy should be to identify the major categories of such conflicts and attempt to achieve consensus as to the appropriate balance between white-collar-crime containment and the other social goals represented by each category.

As the effort moves on to the task of establishing particular substantive goals for white-collar-crime containment, it will quickly run up against the fact that "white-collar crime" encompasses an impressive variety of white-collar *crimes*. Many bear only a superficial resemblance to each other. The question will arise as to how to establish a coherent set of goals for dealing with such an agglomeration of different social harms.

One approach to establishing goals for a national strategy in light of this complexity is to set goals according to the character of the offender and victim, as in Mark Moore's typology discussed in chapter 3. This approach could involve setting priorities for the containment of specific categories of white-collar crime based on their relative cost to society or susceptibility to containment or some combination. Unfortunately, it is easier to agree on this general principle that on is application. Suppose, for example, one orders priorities according to the economic or political power of the offender relative to the victim. Thus one assigns highest priority to offenses by organizations against outsiders, second priority to offenses by insiders against their organization, and third priority to offenses by individuals not relying on organizational affiliation against organizations or other individuals. This ordering raises the question that it may result in the neglect of certain white-collar crimes with important social consequences. For example, small frauds by a proportionately small number of otherwise powerless offenders against a social-welfare program could conceivably gut the program, thus victimizing large numbers of equally powerless people who depend on it. Moreover, ordering priorities according to the apparent power of the offender may be inconsistent with developing a consensus on the need for containing white-collar crime. Enlisting popular support may call for focusing significant attention on the crimes of seemingly petty offenders who victimize middle-class citizens through such activities as charity frauds, home improvement frauds, and the like.

Inevitably, the goals that are set will reflect compromise between competing needs: the need to contain the social costs of white-collar crime, the need to be realistic about the size and the character of available resources, the need to build a consensus among participants, and so forth. That the goals which emerge are unlikely to be simple and tidy should not be cause for grave concern. The fact that goals are set to direct the development of the national strategy will be far more important than which particular goals are chosen.

It is true, however, that the particular form in which goals are set is important. Ideally, some objectives should be stated in measurable form so that the success of the strategy can be gauged as it is implemented. However, there is a danger in exclusive reliance on this form of goal. It lies in the resulting tendency to focus on narrow pieces of the problem (such as convictions) to the exclusion of other important social concerns whose achievement is more difficult to measure. For example, maintaining the integrity of basic economic and governmental processes is an extremely important goal. But its achievement may elude even rough measurement. One approach is to develop "way-station" or intermediate goals whose achievement is measurable and that are thought to contribute to other important goals whose achievement is not so measurable. For example, more frequent audits of financial institutions (measurable) may contribute to the deterrence of embezzlement (less measurable). There are, however, two problems with this technique. First, assumed causal connections may be incorrect or ambiguous. For example, does a social-welfare program whose recipients are never caught cheating represent total success or total failure? Second, once way-station goals are set, they may become ends in themselves while the real goals are forgotten. In any case, goals whose achievement can be measured—whether intermediate or final—should probably not be tied to a specific number. The danger is that too much ambition may result in an overly optimistic number (for example, "increase charity-fraud convictions by 50 percent"). This step could result in abandonment of a moderately successfully strategy as a failure when it does not live up to unattainable expectations.

The Role of Evaluation in Developing a National Strategy

Morrill stressed the important contribution of evaluation to the development of a national strategy. The best social strategies build in evaluation mechanisms at the outset. Thoughtful use of the evaluation element, including ample provision for demonstration programs, can make many valuable contributions. It can help broaden support for a strategy that is working. It can serve to identify parts of a strategy that are not working and help eliminate them. It can lead to the allocation of resources to the most effective mechanisms. And it can help modify approaches that are performing imperfectly. The value of extensive evaluation must, however, be balanced against the problems that may stem from its implementation. These problems include cost, possible disruption of the efforts being evaluated, and the difficulties of assessing results within comparatively short time frames.

The Inadequacies of Current Institutional Structures and
Relationships in Containing White-Collar Crime

As previously suggested, there is an intimidating variety of institutions actually or potentially involved in white-collar-crime deterrence, prevention, detection, consequence reduction, and prosecution. This volume, therefore, has been able to touch only the tip of the iceberg in assessing institutional performance.

Perhaps the most serious current defect in institutional arrangements to contain white-collar crime is the absence of adequate mechanisms for *detecting* criminal activity. Like all other crimes, white-collar crimes cannot be contained unless they can be detected. Unfortunately, white-collar crimes are unusually difficult to detect. Partially this difficulty inheres in the guileful nature of white-collar crimes; partially, it lies in poorly developed institutional capabilities for detection. This inadequacy is felt most acutely in the inability of governmental and business organizations to discover abuses by clients and insiders. The organizations' regular accountants usually lack the skills and other resources to detect carefully planned frauds. And specialists from the criminal-justice system often lack the entree and manpower to act before some indication of wrongdoing arises.

The question becomes what workable alternatives are available. The movement to expand inspector general offices in the federal executive departments is one approach that might be more broadly applicable to a national strategy. Similar offices could be installed in state and local governments. Accounting firms with analogous capabilities could serve the audit committees of private corporations. However, there appear to be at least two limitations to the efficacy of the approach. First, simply placing "investigative" accountants within the organization does not ensure that they will report abuses. Strong incentives such as career advancement will have to be applied to combat the natural tendency to such personnel to become coopted by the organization whose activities they are supposed to monitor and investigate. Second, such extensive use of public and private inspectors for detection purposes might seem to require an unacceptable commitment in dollar costs and in training the requisite accountants, computer specialists, statisticians, and economists. However, such operations probably need not be so comprehensive as to detect *all* abuses. Detection of sufficient abuses to deter most offenders and serve society's symbolic goals might be adequate. That level of activity could entail more manageable drains on social resources.

A still more limited alternative might involve encouraging such operations on a smaller scale than would be required for even a modest increase in the level of detection. Instead, specialized personnel could concentrate on assessing the fraud resistance of the organization's operating procedures, especially those installed for new programs. Better yet, these experts could help design the organization's procedures to enhance their resistance to criminal manipulation. (Of course, the merits of such alternatives will require careful analysis.)

The Role of Educative or Consensus-Building Programs

"Consensus building" has scarcely fewer supporters than lower taxes. The harder questions are: Whose consensus? And what consensus? The preliminary answers to these questions are not difficult to state.

The consensus should be held by the organizations and individuals victimized by white-collar crimes, by others actually and potentially involved in its containment, and by the public. The need for engaging criminal-justice officials representing diverse geographic and functional jurisdictions, officials representing the business and governmental organizations that are the victims and potential containers of white-collar crime, together with a substantial segment of public opinion is obvious. Such support is necessary to tap the ideas, cooperation, and resources necessary to develop and implement a national strategy.

While the base of the consensus should be broad, however, its initial focus should be relatively narrow. The consensus need encompass no more than agreement on the importance of doing the analysis necessary for development of a national strategy. The utility of limiting the substance of consensus stems from the need to sustain the credibility of the undertaking. The need to develop a national strategy should not be sold on the basis of currently soft data on the scope of the white-collar-crime problem, which could be exaggerated. Nor should it be sold on the promise that the white-collar-crime problem can be completely "solved." If either the problem or the government's ability to cope with it turn out to be more modest than advertised, the enterprise could lose the credibility required for a highly effective effort on a more realistic scale. As the specifics of the strategy evolve, the focus of consensus can be broadened to include them.

How and by Whom Should the National Strategy be Developed?

As stated at the outset, this volume served mainly to highlight the important issues involved in developing a national strategy. It also served to emphasize the urgency of the task. Congressional committees, executive departments, and state and local governments are about to take major initiatives in white-collar-crime containment. The time to develop a national strategy is now—

while momentum can be channeled and before major options are fore-
closed. The actual development of such a strategy will require a sizeable and
sustained effort by three sets of actors: (1) sponsors, (2) a senior circle, and
(3) a staff.

The sponsors' function is to give the effort sufficient legitimacy and
visibility to enlist necessary cooperation and support. Such sponsors could
be the federal government through the Department of Justice, LEAA, or a
presidential commission; organizations of state and local law-enforcement
agencies; or private groups such as the U.S. Chamber of Commerce, the
Council on Economic Development, or a foundation, or any combination
of these. The sponsors must, in essence, provide the call for action and provide the presence of a serious and receptive audience for the outcome of the
development effort.

The "senior circle" would give the project its basic direction, monitor
research and analysis, reach conclusions and recommendations for governmental and private action, and sell the conclusions and recommendations to
those who will have to implement them. Those sitting around the table
should probably include representatives of the following groups: the criminal-justice system at all levels, including the judiciary; business and governmental organizations who are the victims of white-collar crime; nongovern-
mental complements to the criminal-justice system such as private security
forces and private investigative auditors; legislators; the civil-service commission; and labor unions. The form of the senior circle could vary along
the spectrum from presidential commission to an ad-hoc group. Something
toward the latter end is probably preferable in terms of actually getting the
work done.

The staff would include the professionals and research assistants necessary to provide the senior circle the research and analysis to sustain the
effort on a full-time basis.

Implementing a National Strategy

Herbert Edelhertz and
Charles H. Rogovin

The NDAA symposium held in Seattle in July 1978 was the first occasion on which so broad a group of representatives of agencies and interests concerned with white-collar-crime containment had been brought together. It was an opportunity not only to consider future directions, challenges, and difficulties but also to concentrate on the barriers that stand in the way of achieving common objectives. Frank discussions over jurisdiction, or "turf," and common concern over resources of money or manpower were paralleled by consistent recognition of the need to find ways to operate cooperatively notwithstanding these difficulties.

It would have been remarkable if subsequent events in the field of white-collar-crime containment had followed some blueprint laid down in the symposium. Needless to say, this did not happen. Nevertheless, federal- and local-enforcement activities in the period that followed were influenced by these proceedings, by the articulation of the issues during the discussions, and by the working links that were developed there.

Planning for the symposium and for the steps that followed it were goal oriented rather than definitional. In the discussions that preceded the symposium, little attention was given to articulating a finely honed definition of the term "national strategy." It was recognized that arguments over definitions frequently stand as a barrier to remedial action, even where there are common denominators among conflicting definitions that could provide a basis for system improvements. It was also obvious that (whatever the definition of white-collar crime) the resources available to contain it are not committed or allocated in the most efficient and effective way. Rather, these resources are apportioned to solve individual agency problems or implement specific agency missions. Thus if a particular agency possesses resources earmarked for white-collar-crime containment, it is likely that it will utilize them itself for this purpose. This will be true even if such money and manpower could be better used by some other agency to achieve a common enforcement objective. Even if a particular benefit program fraud involves both state and federal monies, it is very unlikely, for example, that a federal agency will finance local investigative and prosecutive containment efforts though that may be the most cost-effective way of proceeding. The goal of a national strategy then must be to create conditions in which white-collar-crime-containment objectives can be set, and financial and human resources can be best deployed to achieve containment goals that transcend individual agency interests. This goal can never be fully reached, but there is potential for vast improvement in our present responses to white-collar crime if we can make even incremental steps in this direction.

In the months that immediately proceeded the July 1978 NDAA Economic Crime Project symposium, some steps to develop and implement a national strategy approach had already been launched. The NDAA Economic Crime Project earlier had submitted an application to the LEAA for resources to establish program capabilities to explore and promote integration of local white-collar-crime-containment activities with those of all state and federal agencies. The Criminal Division of the Department of Justice was already working to develop a prosecutive program that would include the establishment of specific units in a number of U.S. attorneys' offices. The FBI was reordering not only its traditional priorities but its very structure to position itself to focus major resources to support containment efforts in this crime area. In Congress the Subcommittee on Crime of the House Committee on the Judiciary, under the leadership of Representative John R. Conyers, was laying the groundwork for an extensive, broad-ranging series of hearings on white-collar crime and on the federal role in its containment. In the executive branch of the federal government, legislation had been drafted to create, in all federal departments and agencies, offices of inspectors general that would be responsible for containment of fraud, waste, and corruption in their operations, procurement, and public-benefit programs. These were not, strictly speaking, steps to develop a national strategy. They did, however, create preconditions, favorable circumstances, and an environment conducive to movement toward rationalization of white-collar-crime-containment efforts. The NDAA project was peculiarly positioned to undertake a catalytic role in bringing these forces together to help coordinate their efforts in development of a national strategy.

Many of these agencies and departments were represented at the symposium and took active parts in it. Linkages among them were to be created in the months that followed, though in some cases they were already developing. For example, then-Deputy Attorney Benjamin R. Civiletti had already met several times with representatives of the NDAA to discuss integration of federal efforts with those of NDAA. Only ten days after the symposium he told the House Subcommittee on Crime:

> I met for, I think the fifth time—concentrating more and more on white-collar crime—with the National District Attorneys Association yesterday in Hershey, Pa. I met with them a month before. . . . I spent two hours speaking to them on this subject and a few others—that the national strategy as it is developed and implemented . . . will incorporate and include their thoughts, their problems, their concerns. . . .

We have established a working group with them of seven to nine major city district attorneys and I think over the next two to three months during the course of this committee's recommendations and studies and longer, we will begin to implement what I have described here . . . the national program.[1]

By July 1978 most agencies that had responsibility for white-collar-crime containment were convinced that enforcement in this area should be a matter of high priority, even if they also had other major crime-containment responsibilities. There was also agreement on the need to rationalize and coordinate the multitude of white-collar-crime-containment efforts. Government departments and agencies responded along two axes. Their first major response was to continue and to expand white-collar-crime-containment activities along conventional lines: obtaining and allocating resources, training, organizing, investigating, and prosecuting violations on an agency-by-agency basis in accord with individual agency priorities. Attention to the changes implied by a national strategy, the second axis, necessarily had to be peripheral to the first. Steps to improve enforcement were relatively clear, albeit difficult; it would not have been possible or desirable to wait to move forward operationally pending the planning and implementation of some ideal national strategy.

Notwithstanding the priority that was necessarily given to enforcement by individual agencies and departments to address their own priority areas. significant steps were taken to further national strategy development. Some were by-products of the need to improve conventional enforcement activities; others represented a direct and conscious effort to deal with integration and rationalization of white-collar-crime-containment activities. Principal among the latter was the activation of a specific component of the NDAA Economic Crime Project. This was provided with financial support by the Adjudication Division of the LEAA in September 1978. Resources were specifically earmarked for national strategy efforts. Though many independent tributary streams were converging toward a common river of national strategy development (a junction still far from attainment), the Economic Crime Project was and still remains the only public or private agency staffed to work toward this goal.

This project had been working for more than five years in the field of local white-collar-crime investigation and prosecution. While it obtained support for this new national strategy development in September 1978, it continued to be responsible for encouraging and aiding the prosecutive activities of white-collar-crime units in approximately 60 local prosecutors' offices throughout the United States. At the same time it has to plan for and lead nonfederal and national strategy-development efforts.

There were few guidelines as to what was necessary, or possible. When

Arthur L. Del Negro agreed to lead this NDAA effort, he had policy-planning support from the Battelle Law and Justice Study Center, which had conducted the symposium for the NDAA and consulting services provided by Nathaniel E. "Tully" Kassack. Kossack had been the project's first director, was practicing law in Washington, D.C., and was a natural link to the Department of Justice and other federal agencies and departments. In his earlier career he had supervised nationwide federal prosecutions of white-collar crime, been a deputy assistant attorney general in the Criminal Division of the Department of Justice, and also inspector-general of the Department of Agriculture. Del Negro was shortly joined by James H. Bradner, Jr., Senior Staff Attorney/National Strategy, who was to concentrate his sole efforts on national strategy development.

Notwithstanding the absence of any clear roadmaps, the general direction of this effort had been clearly set by the symposium, though not by any explicit decisions or firm recommendations that issued from it. It had not been a symposium in any conventional academic sense, in which issues were examined and analyzed, rotated for viewing like the facets of a gem. Nor was it a planning session, in which working designs for future action were drafted. This symposium was, if not unique, at least an unusual exploration of issues, one that led directly to a series of activities and interagency transactions; it was talk that led to actions. These actions were responses to issues that had been raised in the course of the symposium, and were in major part made possible by personal links that developed among the participants.

Del Negro and Bradner drafted their development plans jointly with the staff of the Battelle Law and Justice Study Center. This planning process was preceded by a series of meetings with Mark Richard, deputy assistant attorney general in the Criminal Division of the Department of Justice, and other division representatives. These meetings were initiated by Del Negro because it was crucial that development efforts not be conducted in an operational vacuum. All possible participants in the development process could not be brought together at once. Orderly progress required that relationships would have to start on a more limited scale. Del Negro and Bradner chose to work closely with the Criminal Division of the Department of Justice as a necessary first step in creating working relationships between local prosecutors and federal agencies and departments. In a very real sense, Criminal Division approval was a prerequisite for exploratory discussions aimed at developing such working relationships. The Criminal Division and U.S. attorneys' offices had concurrent jurisdiction with local prosecutors over many of the violations in the white-collar-crime area, and the Department of Justice's position would largely determine the attitude of other federal departments and agencies toward this effort.

During the symposium it was strongly urged that national strategy development be implemented through the setting up of demonstration programs in different geographical areas, and that these be the subject of carefully structured evaluations. In the actual planning of this effort, however, it was clear that this approach would necessarily have to be deferred. While a number of such demonstrations were actually established in six local jurisdictions, they were limited in scope and primarily used to help the project learn about the pitfalls and potentials of federal-state-local cooperative efforts, for example, to develop a cafeteria line of experience that would encourage all local prosecutors to initiate such cooperative efforts and to demonstrate the feasibility as well as the desirability of these efforts. Those planning the NDAA effort felt that it was far too early to engage in demonstrations specifically designed to make possible scientific evaluations such as those discussed in the symposium. In any event there simply were not sufficient financial resources to take such steps, nor would it have been practical or appropriate to prescribe detailed and specific activities for local prosecutive units. The Economic Crime Project staff could lead but not compel local action.

When these national strategy-development efforts began in the fall of 1978, it was clear that the task of developing and implementing such a strategy would be an iterative and reactive process. Initiatives in this direction would have to be internally justified and consistent with the objectives of each agency participating in the development effort, rather than on the basis of a more general goal. All attempts to articulate a comprehensive view of the white-collar-crime arena and the roles of the actors in it necessarily highlighted the complexity of the issues, the difficulties of coordinating containment efforts, and the absence of reliable data on which to undertake policy planning in this area. [See appendix B, testimony of Herbert Edelhertz in Hearings before the Subcommittee on Crime of the Committee on Judiciary, House of Representatives (21 June 1978).]

The basic approach adopted by the NDAA staff and representatives of the Department of Justice's Criminal Division was to work together, in the first instance, in those areas in which there was little or no potential for conflict.

Though the Economic Crime Project staff was not in any position to commit its member units to any particular activities, the new federal initiatives made the time right for creating new cross-agency and cross-jurisdictional linkages. The principal new initiatives on the federal level were the Criminal Division's new Economic Crime Field units, under its Office of Economic Crime Enforcement, and new federal offices of inspectors general in all federal departments and agencies.[2]

The Criminal Division and local U.S. attorneys for many years had been faced with rising caseloads in the white-collar-crime area, which were ravenous devourers of resources. To deal with this problem and to gather data to help the Criminal Division to set investigative and prosecutive priorities, Economic Crime Enforcement Units were established in 13 U.S. Attorneys' offices under the direction of a Criminal Division attorney, Donald Foster. Part of the specific charter of these units was to coordinate the federal white-collar-crime-containment efforts in their areas with other federal agency and local enforcement activities.

Offices of inspector general in federal agencies were created to deal with problems of fraud, waste, abuse, and corruption in their programs or procurement activities. These new federal economic crime units and inspector general offices were obvious focal points for initiation of cooperative and coordinated national strategy efforts. Most white-collar crimes prosecutable by the Department of Justice could also be prosecuted locally; many of the programs that were the concern of the audit and investigative elements of the new federal inspectors general involved nonfederal as well as federal funds and administration. They thus could be investigated and prosecuted by local authorities. These common interest offered the most promising basis for national strategy-development efforts.

The Economic Crime Project therefore adopted a development program, following the symposium, designed to simultaneously improve and construct new relationships with federal prosecutors and agencies, and to use these relationships as a source of resources. Information was collected from local prosecutors' Economic Crime Project units as to the character and extent of their existing relationship with federal prosecutors and agencies that showed, as one might have expected, far more interaction with federal law-enforcement agencies than with federal regulatory, administrative, or program agencies.[3] Particularly effective patterns of cooperative activity were noted between local prosecutors and certain federal agencies, for example, the U.S. Postal Inspection Service,[4] but the general pattern of local prosecutive interaction with federal agencies was spotty at best. Improvement of existing linkages and establishing working relationships where they had not formerly existed were therefore important priorities.

Frequent meetings were therefore held between the staffs of the Economic Crime Project and of the Criminal Division's Office of Economic Crime Enforcement to consider mutual problems and joint training and for the preparation of technical-assistance materials. Plans were made to implement another Economic Crime Project objective, which was to develop a series of memoranda of understanding between the project and federal departments and agencies. These were to give an official imprimatur to cooperative efforts between these agencies and local prosecutors who had jurisdiction to investigate and prosecute frauds arising out of federal programs—and also to enlist federal-agency investigative and financial resources in mutual efforts to contain frauds against these programs.

During the symposium in July 1978, there had been a clear consensus on the need for an office that would have specific, clear, and undivided responsibility for promoting the cooperative and coordinating activities that would constitute a national strategy to contain white-collar crime and that could look beyond its own "turf," or jurisdictional or organizational interests. While every federal and nonfederal agency can genuinely affirm its interest in the development of such a strategy, to follow through is difficult where implementation is only a collateral responsibility for those who have other and higher operational priorities. The Economic Crime Project was provided with such a staff in the fall of 1978—and this staff quickly became the focal point for federal-state-local efforts. It continuously urged its own member prosecutors to meet with and work out new relationships with state and federal agencies. Staff people visited with officials of regulatory and administrative agencies to develop memoranda of understanding and promoted specific forms of cooperation such as joint training. All this led to a meeting in Washington, D.C., on 19 July 1979, which was attended by local prosecutors, representatives of the National Association of Attorneys General, the Criminal Division of the Department of Justice, and U.S. attorneys, federal investigative agencies, representatives of inspectors general from federal departments and agencies, and other public and private agencies.

This July 1979 meeting was, in a very real sense, an outgrowth of the symposium. One year earlier, issues and directions were explored. Now, a year later, agencies and departments that had participated in the symposium and a greater number that had been drawn into the effort afterward, joined together to assess progress and plan next steps.

The purposes of this second National Strategy Conference, cohosted by the NDAA and the FBI and held at the FBI's Washington headquarters, were to inform those attending of National Strategy efforts to date, to assess these efforts, and to plan future efforts. The year between the two conferences had been devoted to planning, opening discussions with agencies, and launching preliminary, exploratory initiatives. While the first conference included participants from the FBI, the SEC, and the Department of Justice, the second conference involved spokespersons from a far broader range of federal, state, and local agencies. There were presentations by the FBI; offices of the Department of Justice (Criminal Division, its fraud section, the Office of Economic Crime Enforcement, and Antitrust Division); the offices of inspector general for the Department of Agriculture, HUD, and the Department of Labor; the Postal Inspection Service; the Secret Service; and the counsel to the House of Representative's Subcommittee on Crime. Other presentations described efforts of HEW and the Department of Transportation. Others participating included an experienced U.S. attorney, a state attorney general; the executive directors of the National Association of Attorneys General and the Police Foundation; two district attorneys with economic crime units; one prosecutor's economic crime unit chief; and staff from the ABA, LEAA, NDAA, and Battelle. During this meeting the participants discussed mutual problems, pointed out areas of interagency friction, and advanced ideas for closer cooperation in the future.[5]

The clearest and potentially most important advance in moving toward a national strategy occurred on 7 December 1979, when representatives of NDAA, of the National Association of Attorneys General (NAAG), and of the Department of Justice established the Executive Working Group for Federal-State-Local Prosecutorial Relations, which has as its stated objective: "to encourage and enhance the efforts of Federal-State-Local Law Enforcement Committees and other forms of intergovernmental liaison."[6] While the Executive Working Group is by its charter authorized to deal with issues other than white-collar-crime containment, for example, narcotics prosecutions, it is plainly evident that its creation is an outgrowth of the national strategy-development effort that has been described. The Executive Working Group is noteworthy in that it was established through the adoption of by-laws (see appendix C) formally signed by U.S. Attorney General Benjamin R. Civiletti, NDAA President Robert W. Johnson, and NAAG President J.D. McFarlane. These by-laws establish specific mechanisms for exploration of mutual problems, exchanges of information, and data collection. Attorney General Civiletti told the group assembled for the signing of the by-laws that:

> Uncoordinated criminal justice services lead to inefficiency. They are a disservice to a public that expects maximum effectiveness from all of us. . . . No one part of the federal, state, and local systems should dominate the others. But it makes obvious good sense to maximize our effectiveness and our ability to prosecute successfully.[7]

NDAA President Johnson went on to sum up the import of the proceedings:

> For the first time in the history of our country the principal elements of the prosecutorial enforcement side of local, state and federal governments will be meeting on a regular basis to discuss topics of mutual concern. It is very important to us who are working at the street level to have a forum in which we can express our concerns about the way in which the federal government is undertaking its responsibilities and direction.[8]

Development of a national strategy to contain economic crime is still in its early stages. It is far too early to assess progress toward creation of an effective national strategy, but there is now a consciousness of both the need for and the general direction such an effort must take. If there is substantial progress toward achieving a national strategy in coming years, this symposium may be credited with a seminal role.

Notes

1. Hearing on White-Collar Crime, before the Subcommittee on Crime of the Committee on the Judiciary, House of Representatives, 95th Cong., 2nd sess., 12 July 1978 (Washington, D.C.: Government Printing Office, 1979) pp. 104–105.

2. The Inspector-General Act of 1978, Public Law 95–452.

3. Battelle Law and Justice Study Center, *Economic Crime Project Unit Interaction at Federal and State Levels: An Analysis of the Results of the National Strategy Questionnaire* (September 1979).

4. Battelle Law and Justice Study Center, *Economic Crime Project Unit Interaction,* p. 32.

5. The meeting is described in more detail in Battelle Law and Justice Study Center, *Report: National Strategy Conference, National District Attorneys Association Economic Crime Project* (B. Hoff, rapporteur) (submitted to NDAA and LEAA under LEAA Grant No. 78-DF-AX-1070, 31 August 1979).

6. James H. Bradner, Jr., "Prosecutorial Working Group Established by NDAA, NAAG and the Justice Department," *The Prosecutor* 15 (November–December 1979): 121–124.

7. Bradner, "Prosecutorial Working Group." Also in "Prosecutor Improvement Program Established," *Justice System News* 1 (no. 1) (February 1980): p. 8.

8. Bradner, "Prosecutorial Working Group."

Appendix A: Symposium on the Development of a National Strategy for White-Collar-Crime Enforcement

Symposium Participants

Mr. Christopher T. Bayley
Prosecuting Attorney, King County
King County Administration
  Building-W554
Seattle, Washington 98104

Mr. Jack Bookey
Regional Administrator
U.S. Securities and Exchange
  Commission
3040 Federal Building
Seattle, Washington 98174

Commissioner Lee P. Brown
Department of Public Safety
City of Atlanta
175 Decatur Street
Atlanta, Georgia 30303

Mr. Scott Coplan
Battelle Law and Justice
  Study Center
4000 N.E. 41st Street
P.O. Box C-5395
Seattle, Washington 98105

Mr. Herbert Edelhertz, Director
Battelle Law and Justice
  Study Center
4000 N.E. 41st Street

P.O. Box C-5395
Seattle, Washington 98105

Mr. James Golden, Chief
Enforcement Programs Division
Law Enforcement Assistance
  Administration
U.S. Department of Justice
633 Indiana Avenue N.W.
Washington, D.C. 20531

Mr. Patrick Healy
Executive Director
National District Attorneys
  Association
211 E. Chicago Avenue
Chicago, Illinois 60611

Mr. James Heelan
Assistant Executive Director
National District Attorneys
  Association
211 E. Chicago Avenue
Chicago, Illinois 60611

Mr. Joseph E. Henehan
Special Agent-Chief
White-Collar Crimes Section
Federal Bureau of Investigation
Washington, D.C. 20535

Mr. Clifford L. Karchmer
Battelle Law and Justice
   Study Center
4000 N.E. 41st Street
P.O. Box C-5395
Seattle, Washington 98105

Mr. Nathaniel E. Kossack
Consultant to N.D.A.A.
Attorney at Law
Perito, Duerk, and Carlson, P.C.
1001 Connecticut Avenue N.W.
Washington, D.C. 20036

Mr. Sidney Lezak
U.S. Attorney
Department of Justice
P.O. Box 71
Portland, Oregon 97205

Mr. Robert Leonard, Chairman
Economic Crime Committee
National District Attorneys
   Association
211 E. Chicago Avenue
Chicago, Illinois 60611

Professor Michael Maltz
School of Criminal Justice
University of Illinois at
   Chicago Circle
Box 4348
Chicago, Illinois 60680

Mr. E. Michael McCann
District Attorney-
   Milwaukee County
821 West State Street, Room 409
Milwaukee, Wisconsin 53233

Dr. Mary McGuire
Battelle Law and Justice

Study Center
4000 N.E. 41st Street
P.O. Box C-5395
Seattle, Washington 98105

Mr. Mario Merola
District Attorney
851 Grand Concourse
Bronx, New York 10451

Professor Mark Moore
Kennedy School of Government
Harvard University
123 Littauer Center
Cambridge, Massachusetts 02138

Mr. William Morrill
Research Executive
Mathematica Policy Research
P.O. Box 2393
Princeton, New Jersey 08540

Mr. Fred Morris
Battelle Science and Government
   Study Center
4000 N.E. 41st Street
P.O. Box C-5395
Seattle, Washington 98105

Ms. Kathleen O'Reilly
Executive Director
Consumer Federation of America
1012-14th Street N.W.
Washington, D.C. 20005

Mr. Steven G. Raikin, Counsel
Subcommittee on Crime
Committee on the Judiciary
U.S. House of Representatives
207-E Cannon Building
Washington, D.C. 20515

Mr. Mark Richard, Chief
Fraud Section
Criminal Division
U.S. Department of Justice
Washington, D.C. 20530

Professor Charles Rogovin
Charles Kline Law Bldg.,
  Room 734
Temple University Law School
Philadelphia, Pennsylvania 19122
  Visiting Scientist
    Battelle Law and Justice
      Study Center

Mr. Daniel Skoler
Director of Public Services
  Activities
American Bar Association
1800 M Street, N.W.
Washington, D.C. 20036

Mr. Edwin H. Stier, Director
Division of Criminal Justice
New Jersey Department of Law
13 Roszel Road

Box CN-14
Princeton, New Jersey 08540

Mr. James Swain, Chief
Adjudication Division
Law Enforcement Assistance
  Administration
633 Indiana Avenue N.W.
Washington, D.C. 20531

Mr. Dale Tooley
District Attorney
924 West Colfax Avenue
Denver, Colorado 80204

The Hon. Robert F. Utter
Acting Chief Justice
Washington State Supreme Court
Olympia, Washington 98504

Dr. Marilyn E. Walsh
Battelle Law and Justice
  Study Center
4000 N.E. 41st Street
P.O. Box C-5395
Seattle, Washington 98105

Session Rationales and Discussion Questions

To aid in symposium deliberations, below are statements of the rationales
for each session, together with a brief list of questions to stimulate discussion. These questions are merely suggestive and are not intended to limit in
any way our discussion.

Session 1: The Institutional Challenge of White-Collar Crime

Session Rationale

Fully exploring the challenge of white-collar crime requires the identification of major social institutions outside the criminal-justice system that may

not only contribute to the white-collar-crime problem but also may play a part in its definition and containment. There are clearly alternative conceptualizations of the white-collar-crime problem with broad implications for institutions and institutional arrangements. Exploration of the barriers to as well as the potential for the interaction of such institutions with the criminal-justice system may identify key elements of a coherent white-collar-crime-containment effort.

Discussion Issues and Questions

1. How, and in what ways, can or should institutions outside the criminal-justice system be redirected or their responsibilities redefined toward effective participation in a national white-collar-crime containment effort?

> Enlisting supportive and cooperative knowledge to identify and respond to the needs of existing criminal-justice and non-criminal-justice white-collar-crime-containment policies.

> Centralizing and sharing the various types of information and the methods of collection to measure the impact and control of white-collar crime.

2. What are the implications of social policies (for example, government benefit programs, tax formulas, protection of privacy, environmental protection) that affect participation of non-criminal-justice institutions in white-collar-crime-control efforts?

3. How can incentives or disincentives be created to assure compliance in major social programs?

4. What can the government and the business and professional communities do to redesign management practices, auditing systems, and personnel supervision to lessen the tolerance of white-collar crime and facilitate law-enforcement efforts?

> Business ethics and professional standards with enforceability, for example, self-regulation supervised or unsupervised by government.

> Screening employees.

> Separation of functions and job rotation.

> Routinely performing pre- and postinvestigative audits.

> Conducting investigations and compiling evidence that requires expertise that law-enforcement agencies have difficulty providing.

Session 2: The Criminal-Justice-System Challenge of White-Collar Crime

Session Rationale

White-collar crime challenges more than the criminal-justice system. Its control depends on more than criminal-justice-system participation. Nevertheless, strategies to control white-collar crime will place pressures on and compete for limited resources in a system that currently has difficulty controlling street crime. Specialized requirements of white-collar-crime containment will undoubtedly complicate the system's pursuit of its goals in prevention, detection, investigation, and prosecution. Therefore, to effectively develop, marshal, and distribute resources to balance the demands for white-collar-crime containment, concentration on a broad perspective is required.

Discussion Issues and Questions

1. What strategies and tactics are available to achieve more effective and efficient enforcement responses?

Reallocating jurisdicational responsibilities (for example, federal versus nonfederal/regulatory versus criminal) for white-collar-crime containment based on characteristics of offense, of offender, and of victims.

Creating mechanisms for case screening that optimize the use of agency resources.

Redefining relationships among existing jurisdictions: areawide *modus operandi* systems, liaison personnel, routinized agency interaction and shared specialized personnel.

Supporting white-collar-crime-containment efforts in nonfederal jurisdictions through provision of federal resources and/or subsidies.

2. What barriers (constitutional, financial, legal) impede the adoption and implementation of strategic and tactical alternatives?

The reluctance of business and governmental institutions to report white-collar crime to law-enforcement officials.

The conflict between stated and political objectives.

Differing organizational objectives, measures of performance, and incentive systems.

Resistance to cede current enforcement authority or to assume new enforcement responsibilities.

3. What mix of criminal, civil, administrative, and private remedies will:

Provide the greatest deterrence.

Maximize protection and benefits for victims.

Satisfy the public need to perceive that justice is being done.

Address current enforcement gaps.

Eliminate unnecessary duplication of efforts.

Overcome the externalities problem; for example, many crimes victimize people in a number of jurisdictions, and no one jurisdiction can or is willing to assume the burden on behalf of all those affected.

Session 3: Meeting the Challenge of White-Collar Crime: Evolving a National Strategy

Session Rationale

Evolving a national strategy to contain white-collar crime will involve many trade-offs and cut across many organizational boundaries. To develop, analyze, and implement white-collar-crime-containment policies, a wide range of policy alternatives must be considered. Reposing exclusive responsibility for white-collar-crime control in the criminal-justice system, for example, would foreclose such consideration and necessarily limit the range of achievable objectives.

Discussion Issues and Questions

1. What are the possible goals of a national white-collar-crime-containment strategy?

2. Are current institutional structures and relationships adequate for containing white-collar crime?

3. To what extent are educative or consensus-building programs essential to the development of a national strategy?

4. What current strategic or tactical program activities and ideas merit resources for experiment or demonstration?

5. How and by whom should such questions as these be addressed?

Appendix B:
White-Collar Crime

Statement of Herbert Edelhertz, Director, Battelle Law and Justice Study Center, Seattle, Washington, at the Hearings of the Subcommittee on Crime (of the House Committee on the Judiciary) to Examine the Subject of White-Collar Crime

Mr. Chairman, members of the Subcommittee:

From my discussions with your counsel, it is clear that this subcommittee is embarking on the development of a long-range examination of white-collar-crime issues that will address the character of white-collar crime, the actors (offenders and enforcement agencies) in this arena, the harm inflicted on our society by such crime, and the character and efficacy of public and private remedies designed to cope with this illegal activity. It is clear that the ultimate objectives of these hearings, which must be to protect our society from white-collar crime and provide meaningful recourse for victims, can be achieved only through adoption of this broad perspective. Such a larger view is particularly important to your task because white-collar crime is difficult to define and, in operation, is often indistinguishable from legitimate activity. The harm inflicted by it can sometimes be exposed only by a painstaking and time-consuming removal of layers of cover.

This subcommittee faces the same challenge encountered by enforcement agencies. To understand and to deal with these crimes and related abuses will involve an exercise that can be compared only to an archeological excavation—the tombs are carefully hidden and constructed with fake passages and antechambers to divert the search. The search itself is so laborious and complex an effort that it can easily destroy the trail it seeks to follow. I respectfully suggest therefore that as you cast a broad net of inquiry through the coming months, you examine the witnesses and the information coming before you with respect to a common series of issues or questions. Preliminarily, you might consider such questions as:

To what extent does the white-collar-criminal behavior described to your subcommittee affect confidence in the integrity of our society, both in the private and public sectors?

What are the impacts of behavior being described, measured not only in dollar terms but in terms of human suffering such as the subversion or destruction of social-benefit programs and frustration of individual aspirations?

To what extent do our laws and the agencies established to enforce our laws offer incentives to lawful behavior and disincentives to unlawful behavior?

With respect to each offense area described to your subcommittee, are the resources dedicated to prevention and enforcement reasonably proportionate to the harm inflicted or losses suffered?

Are there white-collar crimes and related abuses that fall between the cracks because of jurisdictional lines (local, state, federal) or because of lack of coordination along functional lines (police, investigative, regulatory, prosecutive, judicial, and so on)?

Is responsibility for containment of white-collar crime now appropriately divided between the federal, state, local, and private sectors?

Is the business world currently meeting its legal and ethical responsibility to deal with internal corruption? If not, why not? If not, how can it be encouraged to do so?

Is the public well served by the current legal system in which identical white-collar-criminal behavior may be dealt with optionally through civil, regulatory, and criminal processes?

Are government programs that involve procurement of goods and services or the delivery of benefits carefully scrutinized at the design stage to maximize compliance and also to maximize the likelihood that frauds will be surfaced and dealt with?

Is adequate information about white-collar crime currently being collected in the public and private sectors to support assessments of the problems posed and the adequacy of preventive, detection, and enforcement efforts?

The formulation of such a series of questions will, I believe, help to develop a focus that will contribute to the legislative objectives of this subcommittee, to the education of the public whose understanding and support is essential to any white-collar-crime-containment program—and in addition will assist law-enforcement agencies by providing them with added perspectives on their own efforts.

White-collar crime has been with us for a long time. It can certainly compete for the title of the "oldest profession." Ancient tablets unearthed in the Middle East make reference to fraud; there are biblical references to frauds involving weights and measures; commodity-futures frauds were noted in the sixteenth-century Europe; and manipulation of shares of stock goes back at least to the seventeenth century. Our own history is replete with instances of fraud and commercial bribery—resulting in much current legislation as well as the establishing of regulatory agencies at local, state, and federal levels. Nevertheless, it has only been in the last two or three years that the white-collar-crime issue has been raised to a high place in our list of national priorities. This new priority undoubtedly responds to a public mood evidenced by such surveys as the February 1978 Harris Poll, in which 89 percent of the public responded that what they wanted the Congress to do more than anything else was to do something about corruption in government.

One might conclude that this new priority status reflects some greater incidence of white-collar crime. More likely the explanation is that a series of highly publicized events—Watergate, corporate bribery of foreign-government officials, the demonstrated fraud potential of computers—have created a new public awareness of what has always been with us.

I respectfully suggest that this new public awareness may not have long-range staying power, but that it nevertheless does now provide a great opportunity to make a meaningful and lasting contribution to containment of white-collar crime. Such containment may be realized only through legislative and structural changes in the ways in which our institutions, public and private, deal with white-collar-criminal behavior, and from the development of on-going processes for gathering relevant information that will support budget justifications for resources to support containment activities.

What is called for, quite obviously, is the development of a national strategy for coping with white-collar crime and related abuses, a strategy that will incorporate the activities of private and public agencies active in this field. There are steps currently underway to explore how such a national strategy can be developed and implemented, and I hope and expect that these hearings will make a contribution to this effort.

Having made these preliminary remarks, I would likel to make some general observations about white-collar crime. It may be helpful to do this in the form of answers to this series of questions: What is white-collar crime? Who commits white-collar crime? What harm is done by white-collar crime? What is being done about white-collar crime? What is an appropriate and effective role for the federal government in combating white-collar crime?

What Is White-Collar Crime?

White-collar crime is a widespread pattern of antisocial behavior that is financially or materially motivated and affects personal, business, and governmental transactions at local, national, and international levels. It is observable in socialist countries no less than in those that operate under the free-enterprise system. It may be a uniquely difficult form of deviant behavior to deal with because our social and legal structure provides a framework in which white-collar offenders can rationalize and justify their acts.

The search for a definition of white-collar crime has been a fertile area for academic, almost theological disputation. I have suggested a definition that I believe is best oriented to the planning and design of measures to deter, investigate, and prosecute white-collar offenses:

> "An illegal act or series of illegal acts committed by nonphysical means and by concealment or guile, to obtain money or property, to avoid the payment or loss of money or property, or to obtain or personal advantage.

These crimes fall into four general categories:

1. *Ad-hoc violations,* committed for one's personal benefit on an episodic basis. Examples would be tax fraud or welfare frauds. The usual victim is local, state, or federal government.
2. *Abuses of trust,* committed by a fiduciary or trusted agent or employee. Examples would be embezzlement or the receipt of a bribe or favor to confer a benefit. Individuals, businesses, or governments are all victims of such crimes.
3. *Collateral business crimes,* committed by businesses to further their primary (legitimate) purposes. Examples would be antitrust violations, bribery of customers' agents, use of false weights and measures, and sales misrepresentations. Victims would be the public and governments.
4. *Con games,* committed for the sole purpose of cheating customers. Examples would be charity frauds, land-sale frauds, and sales of worthless securities or business opportunities. Victims are the general public, particularly those least in a position to afford losses such as the elderly.

Who Commits White-Collar Crimes?

These crimes are committed at every level of society and in every area of activity. Since the purpose of white-collar crime is to obtain money or some personal advantage to which one would not otherwise be entitled, we are addressing basic human motives, the more insidious because they can be rationalized as:

> *Not being crimes* because the acts involved do not resemble street crimes, for example, bank officer's lending his bank's assets on favorable terms to a business that he secretly owns or in which he has an interest, or padding of Medicare/Medicaid bills by physicians.

Justified since government does not "understand" the marketplace and the needs of business, for example, prohibiting monopolies or restraints of trade.

Need, for example, unlawfully deferring tax payments as a source of operating capital for a business or making fraudulent claims for welfare payments to supplement an inadequate income.

Everyone is doing it, for example, shading on taxes, commercial bribery (corruption in public or private procurement of goods or services).

Thus we will find white-collar crime violations committed by the wealthy and by the poor, by large and small business, in the private sector and by government employees.

Before we too harshly indict our society, however, we should keep in mind that over the years we have blurred distinctions between illicit and legal behavior in the area of white-collar crime, and this blurring has developed gradually. Illicit behavior can be perceived to be less so when society looks on it tolerantly by: (a) lack of adequate enforcement of existing laws; (b) making the same act the subject of optional criminal or civil action; (c) treating white-collar offenders more leniently even after criminal prosecution and conviction; and (d) inadequate concern to provide remedies for the victims of white-collar crimes.

What Harm Is Being Done by White-Collar Crime?

White-collar crimes have impacts that fall into two categories: (a) losses that can be characterized in dollar terms; and (b) secondary impacts, for example, on people, quality of life, business operations, and on the effectiveness, efficiency, and fairness of government programs, and on public trust in our government and private institutions. Many estimates of dollar losses are made, none of which are more than rough guesses. These estimates range from $3 to $60 billion per year in the United States alone, depending on what crimes are included in the estimates and how analysts project actual losses from the comparatively small number of instances that are detected. If one includes, for example, guesses about the costs to consumers and business competitors from price fixing and other antitrust violations, and losses to government revenues from possible tax frauds (many of which are in gray areas of law enforcement), it is easy to make projections (guesses) at or even above the upper limits of current estimates. If one confines estimates to criminal cases successfully prosecuted, measurement of monetary losses are likely to be only a small proportion of the higher figures. Whatever the basis used, it can be confidently stated that monetary losses from business frauds, government-program frauds, consumer frauds, and procurement frauds dwarf into insignificance direct monetary losses stemming from common crimes. However, one should be cautioned against such comparisons between common crimes and white-collar crimes; in *both* cases secondary or human impacts may be far more important. For example, the impact of a mugging is far greater than the few dollars taken from the victim, when one considers the victim's personal trauma, his loss of confidence in the community, and the destruction of inner cities through fear of crime. In exactly the same way the more significant losses from white-collar crime are probably to be found in its secondary impacts that cannot be calculated in dollar terms. For example, how does one measure the loss to an elderly retired widow on a fixed income, who is defrauded of her "nest egg"—which means the difference between a modest, independent life style and dependence on welfare or being a burden on her children?

The secondary impacts of white-collar crime are far more significant than mere dollar losses—no matter how great—because they go to the very heart of the issue of the integrity of our society and to that confidence in our private and public institutions that is essential to their usefulness and effectiveness in serving the public.

Patterns of misinformation, deception, and exploitation found in white-collar offenses can cause severe public anxieties and resentments. The aged are a population specially and cruelly affected. Minorities too are disproportionately vulnerable to such offenses. In its investigation of the Watts riot, the McCone Commission "heard recurring testimony of alleged consumer exploitation in south central Los Angeles. . . ." Not just these particular segments of society feel themselves abused; middle-class persons increasingly seem to feel victimized by consumer fraud and other forms of economic exploitation.

There are other indirect consequences that flow from white-collar offenses. Examples include negative effects on economic development and loss of public trust in established processes and institutions. Banking abuses may dry up the flow of credit to small businessmen and minority groups. Credit abuses divert funds from legitimate outlets. Failure to regulate financial markets effectively has an impact on economic growth and on the stability of private, local, and state government-pension structures.

Many social and economic programs are disproportionately vulnerable to white-collar crime because they lack the powerful constituencies and internal protections of more established public enterprises. Thus welfare programs and poverty programs are often judged by the public and in legislatures more on the basis of relatively small (though not to be tolerated) instances of fraud than on the basis of benefits delivered. Housing for the poor, Medicaid, Medicare, agricultural subsidies, financial support to small and minority businesses, urban renewal—this is but a short list of programs that have been made more costly, have been less effective, and have been deprived of public support because of white-collar crimes.

Other indirect impacts of business crimes require your consideration. Violations of antitrust laws raise prices and distort the shape and direction of our national policies in support of the kind of free-enterprise system we choose to operate under—denying entry to the market for some and rigorously confining the competitive roles of others. Tax violations shift tax burdens. Commercial bribery (for example, payoffs to buyers) not only injures the competitor who seeks to operate ethically but also promotes similar unethical behavior and creates national and international problems, as in the Lockheed case. Enforcement practices, which result in relatively stern prosecutive and sentencing action against the crimes of the poor as compared to enforcement patterns against white-collar crime, create a heightened sense of unfair discrimination in law enforcement that may in fact promote lawlessness and violence. Last but not least, the drive for advantage through the commission of white-collar crime corrupts our public institutions not only through direct subversion of public processes but also through more subtle activity such as concealed donations of unlawful political contributions. The corruption of government and its functions is a major white-collar-crime impact.

The integrity issue is and will remain the most important one posed by white-collar crime. Unless such crime is more effectively curbed, it will continue to erode the moral tone of our society. If it is believed that large numbers of taxpayers are able to successfully cheat on their income tax, those who would not otherwise do so may themselves cheat. If cheating is perceived to be "the real world of business," it is easier to rationalize inflation of an insurance claim or give a favor to a procurement official. If our people believe that there is broad-scale corruption and cost inflation in government procurement, it becomes easier to rationalize false claims submitted to government programs such as those involving welfare or agricultural price supports. If the rewards of cheating in business or violating antitrust or tax laws are greater than the perceived combination of detection/prosecution/punishment, then no amount of rhetoric will very long abate continuation of practices that in the past consistently retarded and undercut our national policies addressing economic, social, and international issues.

One impact area that cuts across the dollar/secondary-impact issue is that of government procurement, on local, state, and federal levels. Abuses in this area present not only an integrity issue but a dollar issue of substantial importance. Bid rigging, false claims, discriminatory awards of contracts that are not justified by some specified government benefit, conflicts of interest that may cause totally unnecessary procurement—all these are of major importance in a period of relatively infinite needs but clearly finite public resources.

What Is Being Done about White-Collar Crime?

There is much talk about white-collar crime but less action in proportion to the scope of the problem.

Our society is currently preoccupied with street crime and organized crime. Fear of crimes such as robbery, burglary, and rape is easily understood. Organized crime, dramatic, sinister, more so because it is largely invisible, seems especially threatening and ominous to the public. These crimes have aroused strong legislative response, epitomized by the Omnibus Crime and Safe Streets Act of 1968 and the Organized Crime Control Act of 1970.

While some LEAA funds have been directed against white-collar crime since 1973 (after the Watergate scandal surfaced and raised our sensitivity to the issue), it has been a relatively small but growing part of that agency's overall anticrime effort.

Local investigation and prosecution have been impeded by two basic problems: (1) lack of resources; and (2) the externalities problem, for example, many crimes victimize people in a number of jurisdictions, and no one jurisdiction can assume the burden on behalf of all those affected.

On the federal level there is a great deal of activity directed against white-collar crime, but this effort is impeded by structural and resource problems.

White-collar-crime containment on the federal level is structured as follows:

Detection of white-collar crime is, with some exceptions, in the hands of administrative departments and agencies. Thus prima facie evidence of any crime must be reported by federal agencies to the Department of Justice, or the justice department's FBI for investigation. In some instances, however, (for example, the SEC or the U.S Postal Service) agencies have their own investigative branches that refer cases directly to the prospective arms of the Department of Justice in Washington, D.C. or to U.S. attorneys in the field.

Most detection is reactive, in response to complaints. Some is proactive, as in the case of those SEC activities that involve monitoring market activity or corporate filings for signs of violations. Other government personnel conduct audits, for example, of defense contractors and taxpayers, but except in a few rare instances (usually to be found in IRS or the SEC) agency enforcement officials are prone to avoid considering cases for criminal prosecution. Agents or auditors alert to criminal issues lose their zeal in a climate of discouragement and delay, or in the course of administrative and civil-settlement negotiation.

Investigation is conducted administratively within federal agencies and departments and by the FBI. While levels of capability vary, they are often quite high but nevertheless have potential for improvement. It should be kept in mind that the arena for investigation is limited by lack of funds, parameters of investigative authorizations, red tape, and concerns about whether and how investigators' work products will be received by prosecutors who have discretion to prosecute or to decline prosecution.

Prosecution (criminal) is invariably conducted by U.S. attorneys and Department of Justice attorneys from the Criminal, Tax, Anti-Trust and Civil Rights Divisions. Where a case is not strong enough or where discretion has been exercised against criminal prosecution for a valid or less-justified reason, the same kind of case may be prosecuted civilly or administratively by other U.S. departments' agencies.

Detection, investigation, and prosecution operate under very real constraints that derive from problems of legal jurisdiction, lack of resources, and enforcement policies. For example, consumer protection is relatively uncoordinated on the federal level, with responsibilities placed in a long list of agencies and departments. Many of these agencies and departments have simultaneous responsibility for policing and also assuring the economic health and public confidence in the enterprises being monitored—with all the conflicts posed by such dual responsibility. Antitrust enforcement is divided between the Department of Justice and the FTC, with each alternately assuming the lead. Sheer chance may determine whether a merchandising-fraud operator will be dealt with by the FTC, where a cease-and-desist order is likely after many years, or will be criminally indicted and exposed to a possible prison sentence as a result of action by the Department of Justice. It should be noted that the FTC has shown great ingenuity in using tools at its disposal, and this comment should not be taken as a criticism of the FTC. Rather, it is the nature of the uncoordinated response to the white-collar crime problem that must give us concern.

Policies are of key importance. Not enough is done by the federal government in contract renegotiation procedures to recapture excessive profits or to utilize renegotiation audit procedures to unearth indications of procurement fraud. Audit and compliance activities within government programs unfortunately often require that numerous review and administrative hurdles be overcome before a case is referred for criminal prosecution or civil recovery.

How we make resources available will often determine whether we mean what we say about fighting white-collar crime. Audit operations of IRS and the Enforcement Division of the SEC, as well as the Anti-Trust Division of Justice are customarily strapped for funds, a situation that must convey unintended and undesirable messages not only to taxpayers, the securities industry, and potential antitrust violaters but also to the attorneys and accountants who represent and advise them.

It is not unusual to hear the judiciary criticized for applying different punishment yardsticks to white-collar offenders as compared to those who commit common crimes. This criticism is valid, but the responsibility must be shared. The courts do no more than reflect the existing overall climate of tolerance toward white-collar crime, as evidenced by legislative, executive, and private policies in this area.

The issue of private enforcement is rarely addressed in considering white-collar crime. Large corporations and smaller businesses spend hundreds of millions of dollars each year on internal audits that could do more (as our courts have recognized) to deter and unearth white-collar crimes. The U.S. Chamber of Commerce, the insurance industry, and other sectors of the business community have mounted investigative and educational programs directed against white-collar crime. The enforcement value of all this is limited by the reluctance of business to refer cases for criminal prosecution, except in instances where no insider is culpably or negligently involved. Corporate officers and their auditors are concerned about their images as competent managers (in the eyes of public and stockholders) if they are seen to have allowed their companies to be defrauded; they worry about liability in lawsuits brought by stockholders on the grounds of their negligence. In more than one instance the fault can be placed at high levels, where corporate officials are involved in conflicts of interest, taking of commercial bribes, and dealing in corporate stock on the basis of inside information. With respect to these crimes, enforcement is limited to detection by happenstance of the vigilance of a particular agency. Internal corporate corruption is a desert area of enforcement—and if there are doubts about this statement, consider how much less we would know today about "laundering of funds" and major secret offshore bank accounts if it were not for the vigilance of a guard at the Watergate building. It should be kept in mind that a program in which government and private industry find common ground in cooperating against white-collar crime can only benefit both large and small business.

What is an Effective and Appropriate Role for the Federal Government in Combating White-Collar Crime?

Most white-collar crimes are carefully planned and executed. They are not committed on the spur of the moment or in the heat of passion. Therefore they are a far more appropriate subject for deterrence than are common crimes.

An effective federal policy against white-collar crime should involve these components:

Setting and enforcing standards of integrity in the operation and conduct of federal business internally and externally in dealing with the private sector (that is, in procurement of goods and services).

Analysis and reorganization of federal efforts to detect, investigate, and prosecute white-collar crime—and provision of resources needed.

Legislative changes to make white-collar crime unprofitable for businesses that are collaterally but not primarily involved in such activities.

Provision of supplementary services and facilities to local and state law-enforcement agencies.

These elements are stated generally and will have to be implemented by specific policies. As a "cafeteria line" of possible items in implementation of these elements, the following should be considered:

1. *Rationalization of the hodgepodge of compliance activities within the federal government.* Every federal department and agency polices itself and its programs, usually through its general counsel, compliance division, or an inspector general. Each such activity should be reviewed to determine whether it is operating (a) to achieve uniform federal integrity goals and not merely internal-agency objectives, and (b) whether investigations are efficiently initiated and their findings transmitted rapidly through unimpeded channels to prosecutive agencies.

2. *Rationalization of functions within the federal government.* Consumer protection is the responsibility of innumerable departments and agencies, banking agencies, HUD, HEW, the U.S. Postal Service, Commerce, FTC, CAB, Consumer Product Safety Commission, Agriculture, and so on. Consumer-protection functions and other department and agency functions should be carefully reviewed to determine whether there are conflicts among duties to those being regulated on the one hand and consumers on the other. The nature and character of the interaction of these departments and agencies with one another, and with the FBI and the Department of Justice should similarly be examined. Comparable analyses can be made in other white-collar-crime areas such as tax and antitrust enforcement and with respect to federal procurement of goods and services.

3. *Administrative and legislative changes.* Statements of public policy, followed by internal directives can have major impact. Much of the federal bureaucracy dealing with enforcement matters has always been responsive to any signals that the executive branch really means business and will act vigorously when called on to do so. Releasing such energies within the federal government will have salutory external effects. For example, a policy of stringent criminal (and civil) enforcement directed against those corporate expense accounts that are merely disguised compensation and against internal corporate corruption will help to change the "everybody's-doing-it" climate, and encourage integrity rather than cynicism within both the private and public sectors.

Statutory tools must also be reexamined. A start has been made on increasing penalties for antitrust violations, for example, but there is much distance to travel along this same route. Victims of white-collar crime should be given greater access to evidence collected by federal investigators. The frequent use of *nolo contendere* pleas by large corporations should no longer be permitted to operate as a barrier to such assistance by sealing information in government files. Statutory remedies should be reviewed to ensure that criminal enforcement is not side-tracked by the availability of alternate civil or administrative remedies that give enforcement officers an easy way out—and thus tell offenders that penalties are just a cost of doing business.

Material resources, as recognized in federal budgets, must be increased. It has frequently been demonstrated that every dollar spent in enforcement pays for itself many times over. The commitment of more resources to these tasks will convey the message that white-collar crimes will no longer be tolerated in either the private or the public sector.

4. *State and local law-enforcement agencies dealing with white-collar crime should be supported through the provision of services and expertise.* The federal government copes with a broad compass of white-collar-crime problems both geographically and in terms of kinds of crimes. Local jurisdictions will rarely be able to support needed banks of expertise, for example, accountants, technical experts, health-care-program analysts, and investigative specialists required for the broad range of violations that nevertheless affect them locally. They will rarely have the investigative or prosecutive manpower to devote to complex cases without injuring their capability to cope with common crimes that are of first priority to their citizens.

It should therefore be federal policy in all areas to develop criteria for provision of more support services to local law-enforcement agencies dealing with white-collar crime. Provision of services is less likely to be wasteful of dollars than are general financial subsidies. There are ample precedents for this in the FBI's crime laboratories, in U.S. Postal Inspection Service assistance to local fraud prosecutors, and in the broad range of investigative, analytic, and advisory services provided by the SEC to local agencies enforcing state securities laws. Heretofore such policies have been a matter of federal agency policy option, implemented by paring already limited resources for this purpose. Such policies should be clearly stated and made applicable to all federal agencies. They should be institutionalized as line items in department and agency budgets. The benefits will be many. At relatively low cost, broad and overlapping state and federal policy objectives will be advanced, coordination of effort will minimize the impact of escapes from one jurisdiction to another to victimize the public, and it will meaningfully convey the message that the integrity of our dealings with one another is a common federal-state-local problem.

I have sought in this testimony to make the point that the test of our nation's commitment to a climate of integrity is what we will do about the harm that is done to our people and our community by lies, fraud, deception, and concealment of the truth in the private and public sectors. There are major and important subissues such as discrimination in law enforcement and dollar costs levied on the public and private sector by white-collar crimes; but these are reflections or consequences, not causes. Analysis and rationalization of our legal and enforcement structure, disincentives to successful execution and concealment of white-collar crime, and remedies for victims of such crime should be the major areas of concern for this subcommittee.

Appendix C: Bylaws of the Executive Working Group for Federal-State-Local Prosecutorial Relations

ARTICLE I

Name, Purpose

The name of this organization is the Executive Working Group for Federal-State-Local Prosecutorial Relations which is hereinafter referred to as the Executive Working Group. The purpose of the Executive Working Group is to encourage and enhance the efforts of Federal-State-Local Law Enforcement Committees and other forms of intergovernmental liaison.

ARTICLE II

Functions

The functions of the Executive Working Group are set forth as follows:

1. Exchange information regarding the use of law-enforcement resources with respect to law-enforcement problems;

b. Exchange information in order to foster an understanding of the different approaches that are being taken by Federal, State, and Local prosecutorial and law-enforcment authorities;

c. Exchange information on legislative proposals that may affect questions of law enforcement which are of concern to Federal, State, and Local law-enforcement authorities;

d. Provide a forum for identifying areas in which additional data will be exchanged regarding law enforcement;

e. Encourage the establishment of Federal-State-Local Law Enforcement Committees or other relations; and

f. Exchange information relative to training efforts.

ARTICLE III

Membership, Size

a. The Executive Working Group shall consist of no more than 18 voting members representing the following three organizations:

1. U.S. Department of Justice:
   (6) voting members
2. National District Attorneys Association:
   (6) voting members
3. National Association of Attorneys General:
   (6) voting members

b. The Executive Working Group may also have associate nonvoting members representing Federal-State-Local and national prosecutorial and law-enforcement agencies and associations who may attend meetings at the invitation of a majority vote of the officers of the Executive Working Group.

c. The size of the Executive Working Group shall not exceed 30 in number including associate members but excluding support staff.

ARTICLE IV

Officers, Staff

a. The officers of the Executive Working Group shall be a chairman, a vice-chairman and a second vice-chairman nominated and selected from each of the three member organizations and to serve for a period of one year. No organization can succeed itself in any one office. No organization may occupy more than one office at any time.

b. Staff support for the Executive Working Group shall be provided by the Criminal Division of the United States Department of Justice. However, the organizations named above in Article III will designate such permanent liaison personnel as may be required to carry out the functions of the Executive Working Group, and such organizations will provide supplemental staffing as needed.

ARTICLE V

Principal Office, Meeting Place and Time

a. The Executive Working Group will hold its meetings at the United States Department of Justice, Washington, D.C. However, the Chairman with the concurrence of a majority of the voting membership may convene a meeting of the Executive Working Group at any time and place.

b. The principal office of the Executive Working Group and its staff shall be at the United States Department of Justice, Washington, D.C.

ARTICLE VI

Committees

a. The regular committees of the Executive Working Group shall be:

1. Concurrent Jurisdiction Committee
2. Legislation Committee
3. Training Committee
4. Committee for the Federal-State-Local Law Enforcement Committee Program
5. Law Enforcement Assistance Programs Committee, and
6. Data Collection Committee

b. Special committees including White Collar Crime and Narcotics and Dangerous Drugs may be appointed by the Executive Working Group to consider and report to it on subjects not within the cognizance of the committees named above.

c. The Chairman and the two vice-chairmen of the Executive Working Group shall, with the consent of the majority of the other members, appoint all committees unless it is specifically provided or ordered otherwise.

ARTICLE VII

Amendment(s)

These by-laws may be amended by the affirmative votes of a majority of the members at any meeting properly convened of the Executive Working Group provided that notice of such amendment(s) and the nature thereof shall have been given to the members of the Executive Working Group at least one month prior to the date of the meeting at which said amendment(s) are to be presented for consideration. Members not present at such meeting may vote by proxy. All other decisions requiring concurrence of the Executive Working Group shall be determined by a majority vote of the Executive Working Group present at the meeting properly convened.

ARTICLE VIII

Practice, Procedure

All meetings and related communications shall take place in an atmosphere conducive to a free, candid, and confidential expression of ideas among members and associate members.

The Executive Working Group is designed to open discussion and to encourage the free exchange of information. The Executive Working Group is not to be utilized as an advisory body for or to provide any advice or recommendations to the Federal, State, or Local Governments.

Members serving on the Executive Working Group shall be designated by the organization the represent. Said designation shall be binding unless and until withdrawn by the sponsoring organization.

/s/ Benjamin R. Civiletti
    Attorney General
    Department of Justice

/s/ Robert W. Johnson
    President
    National District Attorneys Association

/s/ J.D. MacFarlane
    President
    National Association of Attorneys General

                                        7 December 79

About the Contributors

Mary V. McGuire is a research scientist in the Battelle Human Affairs Research Centers in Seattle. She received the bachelor's degree in psychology from Stanford University and the master's and doctoral degrees in psychology from the University of Washington. She has conducted research in the Psychology Department of Stanford University and has taught courses in social psychology and law at the University of Washington.

Mark H. Moore is Guggenheim Professor of Criminal Justice Policy and Management, John F. Kennedy School of Government, Harvard University. He received the bachelor's degree from Yale University and the Ph.D. from the John F. Kennedy School of Government, Harvard University. Professor Moore has written and taught extensively on criminal-justice policy and has been a consultant to the U.S. Department of Justice and the National Institute on Drug Abuse.

William A. Morrill is president of Mathematica Policy Research in Princeton, New Jersey. He received the bachelor's degree from Wesleyan University and the master's degree in public administration from Syracuse University. Prior to joining Mathematica Policy Research, Mr. Morrill held a variety of government positions, including assistant secretary for planning and evaluation at HEW, senior staff member of the White House Office for Energy Policy and Planning, and assistant director of the U.S. Office of Management and Budget.

Frederic A. Morris is a research scientist in the Battelle Human Affairs Research Centers in Seattle. He received the bachelor's and law degrees from Harvard University and a master's degree in public policy from the John F. Kennedy School of Government at Harvard University. He specializes in the analysis of regulatory and other institutional issues in energy, environmental, and national security policy.

Daniel L. Skoler is deputy associate director of the Office of Hearings and Appeals, Social Security Administration. He received the LL.B. from Harvard University. Among his many prior offices have been director of public service activities of the American Bar Association and director of the Office of Law Enforcement Programs, Law Enforcement Assistance Administration.

Marilyn E. Walsh is a research scientist in the Battelle Human Affairs Research Centers in Seattle. She received the bachelor's degree in economics from Wilson College and the master's and doctoral degrees from the School of Criminal Justice, State University of New York at Albany. Dr. Walsh has been a consultant to the U.S. Senate Small Business Committee, and a frequent lecturer and instructor to police departments and other law-enforcement groups. She is also lecturer in society and justice at the University of Washington. Dr. Walsh is the author of *The Fence—A New Look at the World of Property Theft* and *Strategies for Combatting the Criminal Receiver of Stolen Goods* and coauthor of *The White-Collar Challenge to Nuclear Safeguards.*

About the Editors

Herbert Edelhertz is the director of the Law and Justice Study Center of the Battelle Human Affairs Research Centers in Seattle. He received the bachelor's degree in political science from the University of Michigan and the LL.B. from Harvard University. Before coming to the Battelle Human Affairs Research Centers, Mr. Edelhertz was in the private practice of law in New York City and directed nationwide federal prosecutions of a broad spectrum of white-collar-criminal activities as chief of the Fraud Section, Criminal Division, U.S. Department of Justice. His other activities in the public sector included direction of federal interdepartmental task forces examining compliance problems in the U.S. Department of Housing and Urban Development and the Agency for International Development and direction of research on courts, prosecution, and law revision in the Law Enforcement Assistance Administration. Mr. Edelhertz has written or coauthored numerous works including *The Nature, Impact and Prosecution of White-Collar Crime, Public Compensation to Victims of Crime, The Investigation of White-Collar Crime,* and *The White-Collar Challenge to Nuclear Safeguards.*

Charles H. Rogovin is professor of law at Temple University School of Law. He received the bachelor's degree in history from Wesleyan University. Before joining the faculty of Temple University School of Law, Professor Rogovin was in the private practice of law in Philadelphia and held a number of significant law-enforcement posts. These included the posts of chief assistant district attorney in Philadelphia; assistant director of the President's Commission on Law Enforcement and the Administration of Justice and director of its Organized Crime Task Force; assistant attorney general of Massachusetts in charge of its Criminal Division and Organized Crime Section; administrator of the Law Enforcement Assistance Administration; and first president of the Police Foundation. Professor Rogovin has also been a Fellow in the Institute of Politics, John F. Kennedy School of Government, Harvard University, and visiting professor at Brandeis University.